Theory of knowledge

IB DIPLOMA PROGRAMME

Antonia Melvin & Tim Sprod

International Baccalaureate

IB Prepared
Approach your assessment the IB way
Theory of knowledge

Published March 2010

International Baccalaureate
Peterson House, Malthouse Avenue, Cardiff Gate
Cardiff, Wales GB CF23 8GL
United Kingdom
Phone: +44 29 2054 7777
Fax: +44 29 2054 7778
Website: http://www.ibo.org

The International Baccalaureate (IB) offers three high quality and challenging educational programmes for a worldwide community of schools, aiming to create a better, more peaceful world.

IB merchandise and publications can be purchased through the IB store at http://store.ibo.org. General ordering queries should be directed to the sales and marketing department in Cardiff.

Phone: +44 29 2054 7746
Fax: +44 29 2054 7779
Email: sales@ibo.org

British Library Cataloguing in Publication Data.
A catalogue record for this book is available from the British Library.

ISBN: 978-1-906345-21-1

Cover design by Pentacor**big**
Typeset by Prepress Projects Ltd, Perth, UK
Printed and bound by Martins the Printers Ltd

Item code DR43

2013 2012 2011 2010
10 9 8 7 6 5 4 3 2 1

Acknowledgments
Mike Clarke and Julian Kitching for advice on IB theory of knowledge.
IB Publishing, especially Lewis Hamer, for organization, advice and encouragement.
Lou Giudici and Chris White for feedback. Anna Majdanska for personal support.
Catherine Cleveland for feedback. David Cousens for feedback and personal support.
All our theory of knowledge students over many years for teaching us more about TOK.

IB learner profile

The aim of all IB programmes is to develop internationally minded people who, recognizing their common humanity and shared guardianship of the planet, help to create a better and more peaceful world.

IB learners strive to be:

Inquirers
They develop their natural curiosity. They acquire the skills necessary to conduct inquiry and research and show independence in learning. They actively enjoy learning and this love of learning will be sustained throughout their lives.

Knowledgeable
They explore concepts, ideas and issues that have local and global significance. In so doing, they acquire in-depth knowledge and develop understanding across a broad and balanced range of disciplines.

Thinkers
They exercise initiative in applying thinking skills critically and creatively to recognize and approach complex problems, and make reasoned, ethical decisions.

Communicators
They understand and express ideas and information confidently and creatively in more than one language and in a variety of modes of communication. They work effectively and willingly in collaboration with others.

Principled
They act with integrity and honesty, with a strong sense of fairness, justice and respect for the dignity of the individual, groups and communities. They take responsibility for their own actions and the consequences that accompany them.

Open-minded
They understand and appreciate their own cultures and personal histories, and are open to the perspectives, values and traditions of other individuals and communities. They are accustomed to seeking and evaluating a range of points of view, and are willing to grow from the experience.

Caring
They show empathy, compassion and respect towards the needs and feelings of others. They have a personal commitment to service, and act to make a positive difference to the lives of others and to the environment.

Risk-takers
They approach unfamiliar situations and uncertainty with courage and forethought, and have the independence of spirit to explore new roles, ideas and strategies. They are brave and articulate in defending their beliefs.

Balanced
They understand the importance of intellectual, physical and emotional balance to achieve personal well-being for themselves and others.

Reflective
They give thoughtful consideration to their own learning and experience. They are able to assess and understand their strengths and limitations in order to support their learning and personal development.

Table of contents

1. Introduction

"I was so grateful for the guidance that my teacher gave me when it came to TOK assessment. The trouble with TOK is that it covers such a wide area and such huge, life-encompassing issues. When you come to your presentation and your final essay, you can just end up thinking, how can I fit all these questions and arguments into a few minutes talking or a few hundred typed words? I needed to be reminded how to stay focused, be structured and to be selective in my inquiry." (Rita)

How to use this book

The purpose of this book is to help you use the skills and knowledge that you have developed in your theory of knowledge (TOK) classes to prepare for your final TOK assessment tasks. Although this book contains lots of advice and information, it cannot replace your classroom activities, discussions and experiences, or your own reading and reflection throughout your TOK programme. These are essential for building up your critical thinking skills and your awareness of knowledge processes. This book is not a TOK textbook, and we have specifically avoided going into detail about your TOK course.

You will be able to read TOK essays and watch recordings of TOK presentations produced by former IB students, accompanied by commentary highlighting how marks were gained or lost. We suggest that before you read the students' responses and examiners' comments, you try to respond to some or even all of the essay titles by yourself. In the case of the oral presentation, we encourage you to reflect on how you would go about planning and preparing some of the presentation topics which can be found on the accompanying DVD.

What is in this book?

- **Chapter 2** focuses on TOK and the IB Diploma Programme. In this chapter, we look at the importance of TOK as a core element in the IB Diploma Programme and its relationship with the Diploma Programme as a whole. We also explore the impact of TOK as an interdisciplinary inquiry. Furthermore, we highlight the relevance of TOK in your own lifelong learning, drawing on the experience of previous IB Diploma Programme students. This chapter provides you with guidance on how you can use your TOK assessment tasks to evaluate your overall, general learning in order to maximize further the benefits that you gain, not only for your IB diploma but for your continuing education, whether it be higher education studies or an alternative path. TOK can provide you with a lifelong learning programme! Finally, there are details of how each element of TOK relates to other core Diploma Programme areas and how TOK contributes to the overall diploma score.

- **Chapter 3** addresses the question, "What is theory of knowledge?" This chapter is a reminder of the key elements of TOK. Whether you are a first or a final year student, it will help you to revisit the nature and aims of the TOK course.

  We highlight the centrality of the traditional TOK diagram as a way of understanding how knowledge works in your diploma studies. We also emphasize the unique flexibility of TOK, meaning that you, the student, will approach TOK according to your own (and your learning community's) background, situation and interests, echoing the vital role in TOK of the knower and of knowledge communities. Nevertheless, you should also be systematic and critical in your approach to evaluating knowledge issues (KIs) and in your development of analysis and argument, aware of the public standards and constraints on knowledge. Further sections summarize the importance of the ways of knowing (WOKs) and the areas of knowledge (AOKs), with attention paid to key TOK terminology, concepts and linking questions.

- **Chapter 4** addresses the TOK external assessment task: the TOK essay. We give advice on how you can approach your TOK essay, providing kits for unpacking the essay title, and walk you through the stages of choosing, unpacking, brainstorming, planning and writing your final essay. We also provide a full explanation of the TOK essay assessment criteria and how examiners mark an essay.

  Authentic essays and essay extracts follow, accompanied by examiners' marks and commentaries, to show you how marks were gained (☺) or lost (☹). The commentaries for each essay include full explanations of the marking as well as essential advice and guidance on how to satisfy the essay criteria.

- **Chapter 5** introduces the TOK internal assessment task: the oral presentation. We outline the essential stages to consider when preparing and developing a presentation to present a real-life situation and address a knowledge issue that it raises thoroughly and critically.

  We provide you with guidance on how to choose a topic and put together an effective TOK presentation, discussing

the presentation assessment criteria and the way in which marks are awarded to TOK presentations. You can watch real student presentations on the DVD while reading the examiner's commentaries and we show you how marks were gained (☺) or lost (☹) as well as essential advice and guidance on how to satisfy the essay criteria. We also offer guidance and completed examples regarding the two forms you must complete. The completed forms include comments in green boxes to highlight good practice and in red boxes for bad practice.

- **Chapter 6** provides a final snappy overview of your two TOK assessment tasks. We outline the main differences in the requirements of, and approaches to, your essay and your presentation. Use it as a checklist. We follow this with our top tips for the preparation and completion of your final assessment tasks.

Please be aware that there are many good ways to approach your TOK assessment: all that is essential is that you meet the criteria well. This book should be used as guidance only, as reading this book will not guarantee you a high mark—that is down to you. In particular, slavishly following the pattern of the high-scoring essays and presentations is not a good idea. Certainly, picking up hints and pointers from them is valuable, but remember that many other essays and presentations have achieved well by following other patterns and using different techniques. Your ideas and experience are an essential element of your TOK final assessment tasks: examiners value evidence of your own unique "knower's perspective"!

We hope you find this book useful, and we wish you good luck in your TOK assessment.

2. TOK in the IB Diploma Programme

"TOK made me think differently; I found that I learned new ways to argue and write about the things that interest me." (Maria)

Keystone of the Diploma Programme

The IB has described TOK as "a flagship element of the Diploma Programme", or "the glue that holds the Diploma Programme together". As TOK asks you to take a critical approach to knowledge, you could also call it the keystone that binds together the arch formed by your diploma subjects. As a core subject, TOK helps you to engage fully in your Diploma Programme.

> How do you think TOK strengthens the knowledge you have gained in your other subjects?

If you stop to think a moment about the world in which you are living as you study, you will find that its complexity raises many questions about knowledge, such as: What counts as knowledge? How does it grow? What are its limits? Who owns knowledge? What is the value of knowledge? What are the implications of having, or not having, knowledge? TOK is based upon such questions, especially those that you and your classmates ask. TOK will not provide simple answers, but it should provide you with the tools to think and discuss critically the nature of such questions and the issues that they raise. TOK should develop your ability to analyse the information that you encounter and to sift objectively through the evidence for your knowledge. It helps to develop your awareness of the possibility, and sources, of bias. TOK can be a reference point for you and your Diploma Programme studies against a backdrop of ever-shifting change. It is a discipline that challenges you to question the very foundations of knowledge and also to develop familiarity with the varying forms of knowledge that you encounter.

A core and interdisciplinary subject

"It was only when I started really getting into TOK, that I began to make links between the different subjects in my IB diploma. Before that I was just going to classes and doing the work, but TOK kind of woke me up and I began to understand that the subjects that I was studying were all part of the same world, a world that I live in and want to understand better!" (Matilde)

TOK is an interdisciplinary IB Diploma Programme subject, because it applies to all the subject areas possible to study for a diploma, whether it be chemistry, mathematics, history, language A, theatre, or sports, exercise and health science. TOK sits at the very centre of the IB Diploma Programme hexagon, as it gives you the opportunity to reflect upon and evaluate all the knowledge and experiences you gain while taking your diploma. TOK can also be applied to your creativity, action, service (CAS) pursuits, which promote a balance between your theoretical and your practical knowledge through out-of-class activities, and to the extended essay, which provides you with the opportunity to research a sphere of knowledge of special interest and to develop critical and analytical writing skills.

So, TOK encourages you to reflect critically on the world around you and on every aspect of your Diploma Programme studies, and to communicate the outcomes in a focused and critical manner. Your reflection may be spoken, through discussions and oral presentations, or written, in a journal or in the TOK essay. Importantly, TOK will develop your own well thought through "knower's perspective", from which to analyse and evaluate knowledge in all areas of your life.

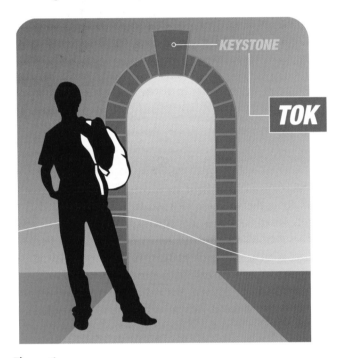

Figure 1

TOK assessment in the Diploma Programme

What does my TOK grade mean?

"It was only once I got my diploma results that the value of my TOK grade hit me—I'd got 3 points [for TOK and extended essay combined] more to help me get into the university course that I so badly wanted to do." (Julian)

The two components of your TOK assessment are the presentation and the essay. Your best TOK presentation score and your final TOK essay score combine to determine your overall TOK grade. Combined with your extended essay grade, this can gain you up to 3 points towards your diploma (see below for details).

TOK internal assessment

The internal assessment component is the TOK **oral presentation**, in which you will lay out a **real-life situation** you have chosen, and identify and explore a **knowledge issue** that arises from it. You will deliver your TOK presentation to an audience of your fellow students. Your TOK teacher will award a score based upon the TOK internal assessment criteria.

There are four TOK internal assessment criteria and your presentation can score up to **5 marks** against each. Therefore, the highest **presentation total score** is **20**. This score can be translated into a TOK component grade ranging from A (excellent) through B (good), C (satisfactory), D (mediocre) to E (elementary).

TOK external assessment

Your final TOK essay, written on a topic you choose from a list of **10 prescribed titles**, is marked outside school by an external examiner against four external assessment criteria, each allowing for up to **10 marks**. The highest possible **essay score** is therefore **40**. Again, this may be translated into a component grade ranging from A to E.

Overall TOK assessment

Finally, you will be given an overall TOK performance grade, awarded according to the band descriptors A to E and based on your **total marks** (out of **60**). So, your presentation makes up one third of your final overall TOK grade, and your essay two thirds. The table below shows the grade bands for November 2008/May 2009, the most recent sessions at the time of writing. (Note that these bands may be adjusted in other years, to ensure work of the same standard gets the same grade, no matter which year it was submitted.)

Total TOK mark	Grade awarded
48–60	A
38–47	B
29–37	C
19–28	D
0–18	E (failing condition—see below)

Be prepared

- It is important that you take note that you are not competing against your fellow students or other IB schools; your grade is completely based on the TOK assessment criteria as explained in chapters 4 and 5.

TOK and the extended essay in a diploma points matrix

The award to you of up to 3 points towards your diploma based on your TOK and extended essay grades reflects the commonality of skills across both, such as critical thinking, analysis, evaluation and writing. Each of these **core areas** is awarded a final overall grade in the range A to E. These grades are then considered together in the diploma points matrix (shown below) to calculate how many points (up to 3) TOK and the extended essay will contribute to your overall diploma score.

You can approach the presentation and essay in one of two ways: as a chore to be got out of the way with as little effort as possible; or as a chance to draw together all the thinking, exploring and reflecting you have done over the TOK course. Pretty obviously, the first is not a good recipe for good marks, but it is also a lost opportunity. Only when you can **apply** the products of all that discussion, reading, thinking and reflecting can you say that you have truly benefited from the TOK course. The essay gives you the chance to apply what you have learned to analysing and evaluating some big issues, whereas the presentation shows that you can consider particular events and experiences, and see the underlying questions and issues they raise.

Be prepared

- Be aware that, as well as developing vital skills for your studies, future career and professional life, TOK can contribute vital points to your diploma.

- Be warned that an E in TOK can put your diploma at risk. Put in sufficient effort to guard against this happening to you.

		Theory of knowledge					
		Excellent A	**Good B**	**Satisfactory C**	**Mediocre D**	**Elementary E**	**Not submitted[1]**
Extended essay	**Excellent A**	3	3	2	2	1 + Failing condition*	N
	Good B	3	2	1	1	Failing condition*	N
	Satisfactory C	2	1	1	0	Failing condition*[2]	N
	Mediocre D	2	1	0	0	Failing condition*	N
	Elementary E	1 + Failing condition*	Failing condition*	Failing condition*	Failing condition*	Failing condition*	N
	Not submitted	N	N	N	N	N	N[3]

Notes

1 If you fail to submit a TOK essay, or fail to give a TOK presentation, you are given N for TOK.

2 Failing condition*: An E in either TOK or the extended essay is a failing condition. However, provided your total diploma score is 28 or more, you can carry one failing condition and still be awarded the diploma. Nevertheless, having a failing condition puts your diploma at risk (if you get 24–27 points, or if you have another failing condition).

3 An N in any subject, including TOK, means you will not be awarded a diploma.

What do you think of TOK?

"I felt that I was going backwards at first. It seemed that the further we went through the course, the less I could trust all the knowledge that I learned throughout my school life up and until then." (Hugh)

If you think back to your first TOK classes, you may remember feeling that you did not know exactly what to make of TOK. However, like most students, you are probably experiencing the stimulation and satisfaction that comes with appreciating the focused challenges provided by TOK, arising mainly as questions that open up your awareness of "knowledge issues": the uncertainties, opportunities or controversies that can be found anywhere there are knowledge claims. As the keystone of your Diploma Programme, TOK challenges you to engage in your learning more fully and with a greater sense of responsibility. TOK can add depth and breadth to your ability to evaluate and respond to knowledge in any area of your IB Diploma Programme.

> Has your study of TOK changed the way you think about any of the subjects you are studying?

Life after TOK … lifelong learning in a changing world

"You can either choose to embrace or to ignore what [TOK] has to offer, however, if you choose the latter option, you will face the dangers of living your life passively. You will let others tell you what is right and wrong, what is real or not. Of course these are never straightjacket answers, but if you take the first option and choose to engage and put energy into the subject, it will also change the way you see life." (Filipe)

TOK not only allows you to make connections between all areas of your IB Diploma Programme, but also offers you tools and insights that you can use to great effect in your later studies and other activities. TOK enables you to develop the skills to support and justify the claims you make and arguments you develop in any field or subject area. The critical skills that you develop through commitment to your TOK course should contribute to your flexibility and integrity, positively influencing you towards a more disciplined approach in every situation throughout your life.

Many students have found that the skills they gained, particularly through writing the TOK essay, have benefited the work they do for their university first degree. Students particularly mention how TOK developed their critical discussion and dialogue skills and their analytical writing by raising their awareness of how to identify and deal with knowledge issues.

In our era of information exchange and communication through the range of media, there is a need for greater assurance of quality and public accountability. We live in a world where sophisticated technical skills in web-based environments are widespread. By developing your critical and analytical skills, TOK allows you to develop your own personal quality assurance "radar". That's what you use when you vet the knowledge you encounter on a daily basis. That's what can also give you the confidence to know that the podcast, video, article or post that you have produced will communicate a worthwhile and well-considered message.

"Another thing that was useful is how personal the TOK essay was—it's one of the few pieces of writing in the IB about your experiences and opinions, and written in the first person, from your point of view. At medical school, I have to write many reflective essays based on my own perceptions, and the TOK essay prepared me to break out of conventional essay format and begin to write more personal, unique pieces." (Catarina)

> Do you find that the benefits of TOK extend beyond your studies in the subject itself?

"It will make you question everything—in a good way—a skill which you will need in order to 'survive' in the world. In fact, it would be true to say that many problems today have arisen from a lack of questioning, of not trying to look at things from different angles." (Hugh)

We feel that greater critical awareness will also enhance your engagement with issues in the world in general. Consider the implications of controversial and world-changing events and information such as US presidential elections, the latest news on climate change or the enormous impact upon world poverty of financial crises. TOK may not provide answers to all of your questions, but it can provide you with the means and the skills with which to formulate and address those questions in a measured and critical manner.

> Can you think of any complex social and political matters that you understand better through studying TOK?

Links to the learner profile

"So much information is available and we depend so much on a professional's knowledge that we have to be able to question the things people tell us. You can't know everything, so you must be critical about the sources you need to use. Furthermore, it's a good practice for other subjects. You learn how to really understand content because you start to think about and question it." (Mingo)

IB learners are:

Inquirers	**Open-minded**
Knowledgeable	**Caring**
Thinkers	**Risk-takers**
Communicators	**Balanced**
Principled	**Reflective**

Through the TOK assessment tasks, you will be able to demonstrate the capacities you have gained in TOK and, most likely, in other elements of the IB Diploma Programme. Both of the TOK assessment tasks require you to **inquire** into knowledge issues, applying your **knowledge**: particularly your understanding of the range of your IB studies and activities. This requires focused **thinking**, and **reflection** about the whole TOK course and how it relates to your wider experience. You will need to be able to **communicate** your ideas clearly. It is central to these TOK assessment tasks that you remain **open-minded**, able to see the world from different perspectives and, even if you don't agree with them, to show a **caring** attitude by taking those views seriously. In forming your own **balanced** view of the issues, you should come to a **principled** stance, willing and able to defend your view. Nevertheless, you should be willing to **take risks**, exploring further the conclusions to which you have already come, prepared to change your mind if there are good reasons to do so.

All these attributes can contribute to your essay and your presentation. What's more, they are attributes that you can carry well beyond the TOK or IB classroom, going out into the world as a lifelong learner.

You should be able to:

☐ understand the role of TOK in the IB Diploma Programme

☐ understand how TOK assessment fits into overall Diploma Programme assessment, and how TOK can contribute points to your diploma score

☐ recognize how TOK can contribute to your overall development as a knower.

3. What is theory of knowledge?

"TOK has taught me that what I think and believe is not necessarily always right and what someone else thinks is often right." (Georgie)

"I have found [TOK] challenging though, because the questions are so open ended, and many do not have an obvious answer." (Charlotte)

Shifting viewpoints

There are many metaphors we can use for your TOK adventure and here's one. Generally at school, your task has been to add to your collection of "stuff"—facts and skills—as your teachers present them to you. You put the stuff in your bag, and get bits out again when you need them. TOK takes a quite different approach: in TOK, you lay out the stuff you already have, and walk around it, looking at it from different standpoints. You reflect on how you (and others) came to know it, and the extent to which this knowledge is good, useful, valuable, insightful or reliable.

You might be thinking we are only talking about your school learning, but TOK aims are much wider than that. You should be thinking about all the sorts of things you know: not just things you can state clearly, but also things you rely on whenever you do something, even if you might not be able to explain them. Potentially, you should be able to explore how *all* your knowledge relates to, or differs from, the other bits.

In a nutshell, the point of TOK is to get you to think about the variety of things that you—and others—know (or think you know). You will reflect on how people came to these bits of knowledge, and whether the claim to know them is justified. In other words, you are being encouraged to become a critical knower, and your essay and presentation are designed for you to demonstrate that you have.

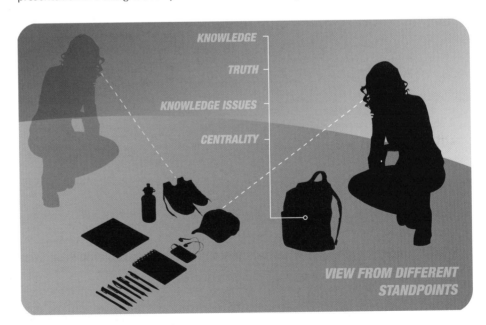

Figure 2

Here's a different metaphor. See yourself as on a voyage of exploration over a sea of questions, with your teacher as captain and your classmates as the crew. Of course the number of questions in the sea is as endless as the scope of knowledge itself, but what is important is that they are asked and explored by **you, the knower**, in cooperation with your shipmates. You, as knower, are central to the traditional IB TOK diagram (Figure 3) because you are central to your own knowing.

Your job is to construct your own personal map of the sea, through visiting the major islands (or key TOK-related concepts), sailing some of the oceans in between, and arranging and connecting them all—to each other but also, most importantly, to your own world.

In your essay and presentation, you as knower will set sail in your own small boat, and will have to navigate your own way according to a specific set of instructions. This voyage will cross only a part of the sea, but your success will depend on the quality of the map that you have constructed while voyaging with your captain and crew. As you get some choice of destinations in these final voyages, it makes sense to revisit places you have previously explored as well.

You are not the first explorer—the traditional TOK diagram provides a rough sketch of the TOK sea, and names the main islands. Consulting this sketch map can help you keep your orientation as explorer, and will provide excellent orientation on the journeys represented by your assessment tasks. You might also find it useful to consult the travel guides—TOK texts and other books—some people have written, provided you incorporate their outlook into your own.

Be prepared

The two TOK assessment tasks are designed to enable you to show how well you have grasped this new way of looking at knowledge. In your TOK assessment, concentrate on weaving together three things.

- A close attention to the expectations of the **assessment criteria**;

- A clear understanding of the **knowledge issue(s)** in your essay title or presentation topic;

- Your **own perspective** as a knower and inquirer into TOK-related matters, applied to your own knowledge and experiences (from in and outside school).

Finding your way

As you know, TOK is a very open course. You, your class and your teacher can approach TOK in many different ways, and consider

situations and problems that are different from those being covered in the next class, school or country. Nevertheless, there is an overall structure to the course, and the traditional TOK diagram is a very useful summary of it, even though it is just a sketch map.

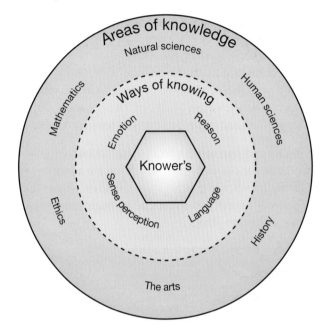

Figure 3 Traditional TOK diagram

Of course, there are many ways to draw a TOK diagram. How would you arrange it, and what would you put in your own diagram of the TOK course?

Be prepared

- You are wise to pay attention to the traditional diagram, as it contains many of the key TOK-related terms which are referred to in the assessment criteria. However your own map of TOK ends up, it should contain key elements from the traditional version.

You as the knower

"TOK opened my eyes and now I see in colour instead of black and white! I now like to talk about things with other people to hear their views (one thing I never used to like to do)." (Jaclyn)

The traditional TOK diagram places you—as a knower—at the centre. This should remind you that, because each person is different, each will look at, understand, reflect upon and argue about TOK issues a little differently. Each knower, and each culture, will spin their knowledge web in a slightly different way, perceiving, discussing, evaluating and thinking about the knowledge issues according to their own experiences. Your uniqueness arises out of your own capacities and experiences.

Written above the door at the oracle of Delphi (an ancient Greek fortune teller) were the words "Know thyself". It's good advice, if you want to know anything else. This is one reason the TOK assessments are such a valuable exercise. They allow you to see how you have grown as a knower, by engaging in two reflective exercises in which you apply to specific inquiries some of the knowledge issues and arguments that you have encountered.

Who you are and how you think, of course, are heavily influenced by the communities of which you are a member: your family, friends, age group, culture and so on. Things that seem perfectly normal and obvious to you might seem strange or even abhorrent to others.

> Can you think of any of your everyday beliefs, or ways of doing things, that might seem unusual or weird to people from another culture or time?

In your essay and presentation, such examples can show your awareness of the ways in which you as a knower have been shaped—and how this shaping might either aid you or lead you astray. Of course, that applies to other people as well. Understanding where they come from may help you to comprehend their knowledge claims, and to judge more accurately whether you should accept their claims.

For, in TOK, we are vitally interested in which knowledge claims we ought to accept. If you are the knower at the centre of your web of knowledge, then you are always trying to incorporate into your web only reliable knowledge claims. Such claims are very often the product, not of your actions, but of outside factors. Many of the knowledge claims you consider in TOK have been produced by structured inquiry in well-established disciplines—the areas of knowledge—and have produced widely accepted, resilient knowledge claims. To reject these, you would need very good evidence or arguments indeed. Other knowledge claims are supported by some but rejected by others. On these, you need to work out where you stand, and why. Be wary of accepting claims merely on the basis of who makes them (though their status and background may give us good reasons to be suspicious of, or to take seriously, particular claims).

Be prepared

- Put **yourself at the centre** of your essay and presentation. Put forward your well thought out views, and defend them. Use your own examples and experiences.

- Show awareness of how you **fit into knowledge communities**. How did you come to be the sort of knower you are? Could you be wrong and others right—or vice versa?

- **Judge knowledge claims** on their correctness, as indicated by good evidence or arguments for accepting or rejecting them.

Ways of knowing

Surrounding the knower(s), the diagram illustrates four ways of knowing (WOKs). You need to be able to talk about what each way is, how it works and how it contributes to our knowledge. For example, the WOK sense perception refers to the way the five senses give us information. Don't be misled by the other meaning of the word "perception" as perspective, point of view, or opinion.

A word of warning here: if you take the traditional diagram too literally, you will be misled into thinking that these are the only four possible ways in which we can gain knowledge, that each of them is completely distinct from the others, and possibly that each area of knowledge uses one and only one of the WOKs. As we will explain, we believe that none of these is true.

Many people have proposed other WOKs, such as imagination. Some of these figure in essay titles at times. The TOK diagram highlights four important ways in which we can come to know, but you are very welcome to propose others. Don't forget to explain and defend your proposal though.

> Can you think of any other possible WOKs you have come across?

The four WOKs interact in interesting ways, and you should avoid presenting them as if they are all totally different from one another. Some examples: complex reasoning depends on language; what our senses perceive can depend on our emotional state; the words we choose might carry hidden but strong emotional messages; our sense perceptions may well have undergone rational processing before we become aware of them. Showing a sophisticated understanding of the ways in which the WOKs overlap and interact is important in your assessment.

It can be tempting to link one WOK to each area of knowledge so that, for example, mathematics is the domain of pure reason, and art involves only emotion. However, a mathematician would not get far without the emotional motivation to spur her on, or the formal language of mathematics to support her complex reasoning. A visual artist needs to make rational judgments about the effectiveness of his chosen techniques in conveying his emotions, and relies heavily on sense perceptions of his subject and his work.

Be prepared

- Have a **clear idea** of each WOK, especially how it works, its power and its possible weaknesses.

- When appropriate, consider other possible WOKs.

- Be aware of the **interaction** between WOKs.

- Know how each WOK plays a role in the different AOKs.

Areas of knowledge

The outer ring contains six areas of knowledge (AOKs). Again, the selection of these six and no others could be challenged: is religion or sport an AOK?

> Can you think of any AOKs that are missing?

Like the WOKs, they do not fit neatly into watertight compartments: is archeology a natural science, human science or history?

> Can you think of any other subjects that seem hard to fit neatly into the traditional TOK diagram?

For each AOK, you ought to be able to discuss the core concerns of the area (what is it trying to do?) and be aware of the methods that it commonly uses both to discover and to justify new knowledge within its domain (including its reliance on the WOKs). You should also be able to make judgments about the significance of the knowledge claims the areas make (how do they change our lives?) and their relation to human values.

Two words of warning. First, be wary of treating an AOK as if it is a single thing. Each contains many sub-disciplines, and the methods of a paleontologist may be very different from those of a physicist, or a poet's from a potter's. By all means use specific

examples, but be careful in claiming that they represent the whole AOK.

Second, try to use more sophisticated examples drawn from the AOKs, rather than very simple ones. Analysing "1 + 1 = 2" as an example of mathematics, or "water boils at 100°C" as an example of the natural sciences will miss much that is distinctive and important about those AOKs. It would be better to analyse the derivation of the roots of a quadratic equation, or the replacement of the idea that the continents are fixed with plate tectonics. You are studying subjects from most—perhaps even all—of the AOKs at quite a high level in your Diploma Programme, so draw on your own studies for authentic examples.

Be prepared

- Have a **clear idea** of each AOK, its methods, significance and limitations.

- Be aware that **subjects** within an AOK **can be different** in various ways or even **overlap** several AOKs.

- Use **interesting, relevant and** (where possible) **authentic examples** to help you explain and analyse the AOKs.

TOK-related terms and concepts

There's not much point talking about knowers, WOKs or AOKs without clarifying what **knowledge** itself is. "Knowledge" is a TOK-related term: indeed it is the chief one. These terms form an essential vocabulary for doing TOK, because they stand for the key concepts of TOK. Of course, these key concepts can often be explained using more simple words. Indeed, that will be important in your assessment tasks: that you can make clear what these key TOK terms mean, rather than just throw in the "big words" without explanation. When it comes down to it, if you can explain the concept without using the term, you will do better than if you use the term without showing you understand it.

Like other TOK-related terms, "knowledge" marks a contestable concept. People disagree about exactly what counts as knowledge, and how it relates to other concepts such as belief, opinion, information and so on. In your assessment tasks, where appropriate, you must make clear and defend the particular meaning you will give to such key terms. For example, you could contrast those who claim "only beliefs that are true count as knowledge" with those who think "knowledge is what fits in with my other knowledge".

It is impossible to give an exact list of all the TOK-related terms. They are the ones that come up often in a wide range of TOK discussions, because they are central to TOK-type thinking. Of course, you can't discuss every word you use, every time. Often, even TOK-related terms can be used in a consistent, commonly accepted way, when their exact meaning is not critical to the discussions. However, you must be careful with the terms that are central to your argument. We have already used quite a few of them, such as belief, culture, experience, intuition, truth, values. They are often found in essay titles, and can be essential to your development of the presentation. Beware of relying on dictionary definitions for their meaning. Dictionaries merely point towards the meaning, for those who are unfamiliar with the word. TOK-related terms, though, are contestable: their meaning is subject to much disagreement, and so is not obvious. A dictionary cannot capture them.

So, do not loosely use TOK-related terms that are central to your essay or presentation. Make clear what you take the term to mean, justify your decision and stick to it. Don't slide between different accounts of them (for example, from truth as "what matches the world", to truth as "what everyone believes"). When you do consider other possible meanings of them, mark this clearly by using phrases such as "on the other hand" or "an alternative view is …".

Be prepared

- Be careful with key **TOK terms**. Define them carefully and use them consistently. Don't just throw them in without an explanation.

- Show your awareness of **different views** of what they mean.

- **Beware of sliding** between different, incompatible, meanings.

- In most cases, **avoid dictionary** definitions. If you have a good case for using one, do it with care.

Knowledge issues

Finally, we turn our attention to the phrase **knowledge issues**. Despite not appearing on the TOK diagram, it is a key term, which you need to understand in order to be able to do well in the assessment tasks. It appears in three of the four assessment criteria for both the presentation and the essay. So, what does TOK mean by "knowledge issues"?

Knowledge issues arise from **knowledge claims**. We all make knowledge claims, every time we claim to know something. There are many different types: for example, they may be specific or general, concrete or abstract, explicit or implicit.

To use some specific claims as examples, people may explicitly say "Bangkok is in Thailand" or "I know how to cook cassava so it is not poisonous". Or they may just act on implicit (unspoken)

knowledge, by applying for a Thai visa when they book the Bangkok flight, or by cooking the family a cassava meal.

To use more general examples, knowledge claims can be widely accepted, such as "A force of attraction exists between any two material objects", or very contentious, such as "Modern art is more meaningful than Renaissance representative art".

Most of us regularly search out new knowledge claims, be they to answer questions personal ("What career would suit my strengths and interests?") or public ("What policies would best balance the need for jobs with the demands of the environment?"). Much of your schooling is about increasing the number of knowledge claims you can make and act on.

However, in TOK, unlike in your other Diploma Programme subjects, your aim is not primarily to discover or learn new knowledge claims (though you will learn some). Rather, TOK is essentially concerned with **examining** the knowledge claims that you or others make, to answer queries about the status of those claims. Any issues that arise when we do this are knowledge issues.

Be prepared

- A knowledge issue is an inquiry that arises from wondering about the status of one of our knowledge claims. It often arises from a question that could start with "How can we know … ?"

When you are trying to write about the knowledge issue that is going to form the centre of your essay or presentation, the senior TOK examiners have given you some advice. They say that a good knowledge issue for assessment purposes will be an open-ended question that is explicitly about knowledge itself, and is written to raise the relationships between that knowledge and other TOK terms.

Any knowledge claim may give rise to many knowledge issues. In the following table, we give some examples of knowledge claims and, for each, an example of a knowledge issue that can arise from it.

Many (but not all) knowledge issues can be reworded to start "How can we know … ?" This can be a good test of whether your issue is a knowledge issue or not.

> How would you rephrase the knowledge issues in the table opposite?

Of course, it is one thing to identify a knowledge issue, and another to deal with it: advice on the latter is the subject of much of the rest of this book.

Knowledge claim	Possible knowledge issue
Wikipedia says that Bangkok is in Thailand.	How can I use reason to know whether information from an internet source is accurate and reliable?
My mother says that she can show me how to cook cassava so it is not poisonous.	When should I believe folk knowledge that has not been scientifically tested?
A force of attraction exists between any two material objects.	Why should we believe a general scientific law when we have not tested every instance?
Modern art is more meaningful than Renaissance representative art.	What are the criteria we can use to distinguish more meaningful art from less meaningful?
My eyes tell me that this stick bends when it goes into the water.	How can we know when our senses are giving us accurate information about the world?
There can be no knowledge without emotion … until we have felt the force of the knowledge, it is not ours.	What impact do our emotional states have on our gathering of knowledge, and on the knowledge we gather?
Shakespeare tells us that Richard III was a cruel, ruthless man.	In what ways does literature tell the truth: about historical events, or about the way human beings are?
People in country X jail homosexuals; people in country Y allow them to marry.	Does the fact that different societies have opposing moral views mean that there is no absolute moral truth?
Being educated means learning to see through the clichés of my society.	In what ways do common beliefs in a society help and hinder us in finding the truth?
My homeopath says the contents of this bottle will cure me, but my doctor says they will do nothing at all.	How reliable are scientific methods when used to test apparently incompatible claims about how the world works?
The choice of the phrase "all men are created equal" instead of "all humans …" set back women's rights 200 years.	To what extent does the choice of words to express ideas subconsciously alter our understanding of them?
I saw a video last night that proves that global warming is a swindle.	What emotional techniques do documentary makers use to shape our judgments about experts' claims to knowledge?

You should be able to:

☐ understand the aims and purpose of TOK

☐ recognize the main elements of the TOK course: knower(s), ways of knowing, areas of knowledge, TOK terms and concepts

☐ identify and write down knowledge issues.

4. The TOK essay

"Once I got used to theory of knowledge, I enjoyed writing the essays because I found that they were an opportunity for me to think for myself about the way I was building up my knowledge and values. Writing a TOK essay was my 'me space' for reflecting on a very wonderful but confusing world of knowledge and issues around me and to decide what is and what is not most important. My final essay was a chance to calmly evaluate some of the knowledge I'd discovered on my diploma!" (Isobel)

Unpacking a strange bag

We have described the TOK course as a voyage over the sea of knowledge. Now, we will liken the two TOK assessment tasks to two different types of bags for the voyage. The essay title can be understood to be a bag of things provided to you. Each title, then, is like a bag provided for your convenience by a shipping company. This bag will contain somebody else's idea of essential articles for your voyage, such as toiletries, soap or shampoo. Your job is to unpack the bag, identify its contents, and then build a display (your essay) that explains how the bag's contents can be understood in terms of, and applied to a part of, the knowledge sea. The TOK prescribed titles are a collection of 10 bags from which you must try to choose the one that is best for you. A bag provided by a stranger might at first seem strange but, on opening it, you will soon find items that are familiar to you, like those in the bag described above.

Figure 4

The essay process

You might be tempted to grab the first likely looking title and start writing, but we suggest that you approach the task in five stages:

Unpack the 10 titles ➡ **Choose** your title ➡ **Brainstorm** the elements to include ➡ **Plan** out the essay ➡ **Write** the essay

We will concentrate mostly on the first three of these stages for two reasons. First, we believe that, if you unpack the titles carefully, choose the one that suits you best and brainstorm what to include well, then you are very likely to do a good job of the planning and writing. Second, we can offer general procedures for these first three, but how to plan and write your essay will depend quite a lot on the details of your unpacking and brainstorming.

Unpacking the titles

Before choosing your TOK essay title bag, you will need to know what each of them contains. The 10 titles offered cover a range of focuses and styles, each indicating different knowledge issues and inviting different considerations when you write your essay. Although the outward appearance of some of the titles may appear daunting at first, you will find when you unpack the "bag" and look more carefully that you come across very familiar TOK contents such as the AOKs, the WOKs, the attributes of knowers, or key TOK concepts such as certainty, reliability, truth, validity, context or culture. It makes sense to take a careful look through the 10 title "bags" and pick the one that suits you and your understanding of TOK best. Don't choose a bag whose contents are unfamiliar to you!

Know what can be found in titles

To begin unpacking a title, you need to open the bag and turn out the items that you find inside. You then need to identify which items are essential ones. Just as any bag would have features that allow us to identify it as a bag, all TOK essay titles share basic features with other titles. They all:

- arise from the TOK course

- contain references to key TOK elements (AOKs, WOKs, and/or TOK-related terms)

- contain action terms (words that indicate to you what your task is)

- point to or state knowledge issues

- allow different, equally valid, approaches in the essay.

In addition, some allow a certain amount of ambiguity in how

the title (or some key term) is to be understood, or are based on certain assumptions with which you may not agree.

Unpacking the title means examining, clarifying and exploring all these central items in each particular title. Later in this chapter, as exemplars, we take you through a process of unpacking the essential features and requirements of five essay titles from the November 2007–May 2008 prescribed title list. We will also illustrate the brainstorming phase, and provide you with actual essays and essay extracts (written by previous students), accompanied by commentaries to show how marks were gained and lost.

Many of our unpacking suggestions can be applied to any TOK essay title, whereas others are more pertinent to certain titles. Therefore, we also take you through the more individualized aspects of each essay title type. You can then apply our guidelines to unpacking, choosing, brainstorming, planning and writing your own essay. As not all bags are identical, neither are all TOK essay titles. We will identify several different common essay types in the next section. Knowing which essay type you have chosen will help you apply these guidelines to your particular essay title.

Essay types

Many essays will fall into one of four different types with somewhat different emphases. Recognizing the type may assist you to unpack, address and answer the prescribed title. Below we give you examples of the four types from previous prescribed title lists.

1. Titles that focus on a TOK-related term (or two), asking for evaluation across AOKs and/or WOKs.

   "When mathematicians, historians and scientists say that they have explained something, are they using the word 'explain' in the same way?" (Title 1, 2006–7)

   TOK-related term: explain. AOKs: mathematics, history, natural science.

2. Titles that focus on an area of knowledge (or maybe two) and require comparison or contrast between AOKs or across WOKs, generally looking at a TOK-related term (or two).

   "It is often claimed that scientific results must be replicable.

Is this possible or desirable in other areas of knowledge?" (Title 2, 2006–7)

AOK: natural science. Other AOKs: your choice. TOK-related term: replicable.

3. Titles that focus upon a way of knowing (or maybe two), and require comparison with other WOKs or across AOKs, generally looking at a TOK-related term (or two).

"Some people say that religious beliefs can be neither justified nor refuted by reason. However, while sometimes this claim is used as a reason for rejecting religious beliefs, at other times it is used to conclude that these beliefs are established by faith. To what extent is faith a legitimate basis for knowledge claims, in religion and different areas of knowledge?" (Title 7, 2005–6)

WOK: reason. Other AOKs: religion, your choice. TOK-related terms: faith, belief.

4. Titles that focus on an example, quote or general statement, to be explored by reference to AOKs and/or WOKs and/or TOK-related terms.

"There are many different authorities, including academics, politicians, global organizations and companies, who make knowledge claims. As an experienced TOK student, what criteria do you use to distinguish between knowledge, opinion and propaganda?" (Title 1, 2005–6)

General statement: authorities making knowledge claims. AOKs/WOKs: your choice. TOK-related terms: knowledge, opinion, propaganda.

Remember these types, as they will be referenced later in the book.

Be prepared

- Systematically unpack each title, so that you know what it would require of you, if you chose it.

- Be aware of different types of title, to help with the unpacking.

Choosing the title

"I couldn't believe how difficult it was for me to choose a final title, but when I started to think about what I wanted to bring into my essay and what arguments I would enjoy developing, then I was able to make that choice." (Pedro)

In picking your title, you are looking for the best match of three things: the demands of the title, the map of TOK you have developed through your TOK course, and yourself as a knower

with certain interests and attributes. Your unpacking of the title will have revealed to you the first. A backward look at your TOK course should show you the knowledge issues in which you have gained experience and developed an interest throughout your TOK course. Reflecting on yourself as a knower, you will have discovered what style of knowing and learning you have gained through your school experiences and your everyday life. Some essays will appeal more to your interests, experience and concerns. To help you choose your essay title, here is a selection of useful questions that you can ask yourself.

- What does each title want you to do?

- Do any of the titles link strongly to matters that your class covered in depth and detail?

- Do any of the titles suit your style of learning, for example, by requiring a more critical and rational, or a more creative and imaginative, approach?

- Would any of the titles allow you to focus on your academic strengths and interests, for example, the AOKs you are doing at higher level?

- Would any of the titles allow you to focus on the WOKs that you prefer to use to gain knowledge?

- For any of the titles, could you draw on your extended essay research, or your CAS activities?

- Would any of the titles allow you to focus on activities and projects that interest you outside school?

> What other considerations might help you to choose the best title for you?

Be prepared

- Read carefully through the list of 10 prescribed titles. Unpack each to work out what it is asking you to do.

- Discard the titles you definitely do not want to answer.

- Decide which of the remaining titles interests you the most and suits you the best.

Brainstorming

Now you have unpacked and chosen your "title bag", what next? Clearly, your eventual aim is to write an essay of between 1,200 and 1,600 words on the title, but we strongly suggest that you do not begin writing straight away. Rather, you ought to brainstorm for ideas, and then arrange those ideas into a coherent plan. Writing the essay will then be much easier—and the essay will be better too.

You can think of your essay as your own designer bag, especially devised by you. Your "essay bag" will have several features. It will be much bigger and more transparent than the title bag that you originally unpacked. You will need to fit into your own essay bag the key items from the title. Each will need to be accompanied by a lot of new items you will supply, such as explanations, explorations, argumentation and examples. It will also have to invite the viewer to see the items from different perspectives, and it will need to contain some counter-arguments. Where will all these come from?

First, we urge you to look back at the way you unpacked the title. Rummage around inside the title again: did you overlook any important contents? Have you figured out which are the key terms from TOK, what the action terms are asking you to do, what the knowledge issue is that you will address, whether the question is ambiguous, whether it makes assumptions you will want to question?

Now, extend your unpacking by brainstorming ideas related to these items. A brainstorm is a time for gathering together items that **might** be useful in your essay. You can start by jotting down ideas related to the items you pulled out of the title bag.

- How will you use the key terms—what meanings will you have for them?

- What is the knowledge issue for your essay? Exactly how might you word it?

- How will you make sure you achieve the tasks demanded by the action terms?

- What exactly does the title mean to you? How can you explain this to others?

- What ambiguity might the title contain? How will you interpret it?

- If there are any assumptions in the title, will you agree with, or question, them?

Next, brainstorm ways of developing your essay. If you have identified AOKs, WOKs and/or key TOK-related terms from the title, good. If they are your choice, which are you going to use? What points will you make concerning them? What examples might you use to explain them? Are there counter-examples? Counter-arguments? How could you introduce different perspectives? Most importantly, what will be your basic answer to the title and its knowledge issue—that is, your major line of argument? You should be aiming to be able to write this in a sentence.

A word of advice on this line of argument. You should come to a definite answer to the title. This does not mean that your answer has to be "yes, definitely" or "no, never". Often, it will be more along the lines of "yes, in some cases, under these circumstances, but no in these other cases" (or some other answer that recognizes complexity). We feel strongly that it should never be "who knows?" or "it all depends on your opinion".

Note that it is by no means essential to follow the order we have used. Brainstorming any one of these items may bring to mind possible items of a different sort. In particular, gathering items will help you develop your ideas on your basic line of argument, which in turn will suggest to you further ideas for the other items. Jot them all down, using whatever method works for you—scribbling on paper, using a mind map, typing onto a computer, or any other way. You are aiming to have many possible contents for your essay bag laid out in front of you, for the next stage: planning.

Planning your essay

"I found writing the essay was both like unravelling a ball of wool or making a collage, it was about analysing and argumentation, but it was also far more creative than I imagined it would be!" (Mia)

Design your own bag

You have now gathered a jumbled pile of items for your essay bag; what are you going to do with them? To guide your planning, you will need to have a unifying design. The contents of the bag will need to be organized so that they are clearly visible and accessible. The bag will also need to be stitched together well, to carry the weight, as you develop depth and breadth in your essay. Although your essay will be uniquely yours, there are general design specifications that it will need to meet. Apart from the essay title, these specifications are contained in the essay criteria (which we consider below).

While you were doing your brainstorming, you will have been thinking about your line of argument. Sometimes, this will come to you early in the process above, and help guide your brainstorming. Sometimes, it only emerges when you have gathered much other material. Now that you have a good idea of items that might go into your bag, this line of argument is what you will use as your unifying design. Guided by your line of argument, rearrange the items you have gathered into a plan, which leads from an introduction that clarifies how you understand the title and its demands, through a carefully constructed argument, to a conclusion that draws it all together. To meet the title specifications, you need to be very clear about the nature of the objects that you find in the title bag. Which are the essential items? How can they be best displayed? What other items will you need to add to the collection, and where? Good planning will ensure that your new bag is well designed in order to hold, carry and display the items effectively.

Although we have offered you some general rules for unpacking, brainstorming and planning a designer essay in response to the prescribed title you chose, it is up to you to fill in the details of the design, drawing on your own experiences, interests, general knowledge and IB studies. Having a good design for your essay—an essay plan—is essential if you want a bag that is as strong and useful as it is eye-catching!

Be prepared

- Before writing your essay, develop notes, a diagram or something similar, in which your plan for organizing your ideas is clearly laid out.

- Make sure the main ideas, including your knowledge issue and line of argument, are obvious.

- Show your plan to others—at the very least, to your teacher.

Writing to the assessment criteria

"In my final year, my teacher went through the criteria with us and I made sure that I had a copy by me whilst I wrote my essay. It was like using a recipe!" (Inés)

Constructing a useful bag

Since all TOK essays are marked according to the essay assessment criteria, these criteria should be your constant companions. If you are familiar with the TOK essay assessment criteria, you will be more focused and organized in planning and developing your essay. They should give you a clear idea of the essential considerations to have in mind. If your essay is a bag, the criteria are the general guidelines that apply to all well-constructed bags.

We have previously claimed that TOK is like a voyage on a sea of knowledge complexities and controversies. As you journeyed on the TOK voyage through knowledge issues, you have discovered and collected many ideas, insights and messages, and kept them as notes, journal entries, memos, reflections, text extracts or other items. These are a rich collection of your ideas and examples. You now need to locate and access the relevant records in order to construct your essay.

To guide yourself in constructing your bag, study the essay assessment criteria. They can help you to select and organize the complex collection of issues and ideas that you want to address

in your TOK essay. You can think of the criteria as rules for bag making that you can follow to guide the way you assemble the bag. A craftsperson would examine each rule carefully. Like that artisan, regard the TOK criteria as vital guidelines to study and evaluate carefully in order to be very clear about their focus. Remember, the external examiner will use them to mark your TOK essay. We recommend that you make your own summary, to have on hand as you write. If used wisely, the criteria will lead firmly to the final goal—your completed TOK essay!

The essay assessment criteria

Criterion A assesses to what extent your essay shows that you **understand** the **knowledge issue** or knowledge issues directly related to the essay title.

- When you unpack the title, you should **identify** the knowledge issue(s) related to the essay title. Sometimes, the essay title makes the KIs very clear: for example "Are reason and emotion equally necessary in justifying moral decisions?" At other times, the central KIs are **less explicit**: for example "Evaluate the role of intuition in different areas of knowledge." This title is more open to interpretation and there are several KIs, including:

  - What is the nature and status of intuition in the creation of knowledge?

  - Does intuition have a role to play in [several named AOKs]?

  - If intuition enables knowledge to be gained within AOKs, is it in fact another WOK?

  Either way, **state** the KI you will be addressing explicitly.

- Show your **understanding** of the KI raised by the title through your own expression and perspectives. However, be careful to **address** explicitly the KIs raised by the question. If you do not, your essay will be of a lower standard.

- Of course you can address several KIs, but the order and manner in which you do so will depend upon the **approach** and **perspectives** taken by you, the knower.

- **Use your introduction** to lay out clearly what you take the KIs to be, in your own words: parroting or repeating the title does not show the reader anything. If you are going to focus on a KI raised by the title, but not explicitly stated by it, you need to show the connection between your essay and the title.

- Show both **depth** and **breadth** in your treatment of the KIs, by discussing the nature of knowers, the WOKs and the AOKs and so on—but only to the extent that you can show they are relevant to the title. "Name-checking", or just making sure that TOK terms get mentioned, is not enough. For example, for some titles it might be appropriate to mention all the WOKs, but for others this might not. **Unpacking** the title well and **planning** carefully will have told you which WOKs you will address, and how you will show that they are relevant.

- To **demonstrate depth**, carefully and systematically **explore** and **analyse** one (or usually more) of the WOKs or AOKs. Show how KIs related to this/these WOKs/AOKs are connected to the title. For example, you might show how natural sciences come up with the conclusion that a table is mostly empty space, or what the essential features of language are, as you are going to use the term.

- **Display** your breadth of understanding by **comparing** and **contrasting** two (or more) WOKs or AOKs in one or more respects, taking note of the particular focus of the title. In that respect, explain how the two are **different** or **similar**. For example, you might discuss how investigative work in science and many valuable works of art both follow and confirm well-established conventional methodologies. However, ground-breaking work is different: radical new art such as some graffiti or conceptual art and revolutionary scientific theories such as quantum theory break conventions. They show how certain concepts or ideas can be understood better by taking a different approach or by making a paradigm shift.

- Overall, you will address criterion A best if you write an essay with well thought out and systematically presented detail. **Do what you do well**, aiming at depth rather than trying to cover too many WOKs and AOKs.

Criterion B is all about your **knower's perspective**, which is, as we have seen, central to your whole understanding of TOK and certainly important in your essay. For this criterion, you have several main, interrelated, tasks. You need to show that you can:

- **think for yourself** about the title's concerns (rather than just copying what others—your teacher, your TOK text, a book you read—may say)

- **link** your own life and experience as a learner to the knowledge issues that you have identified

- **be aware** of how your own viewpoint has been shaped by your own features (such as gender, social setting or type of education)

- **consider** how there may be multiple perspectives and how the issue might be approached differently (for example, by a person from a different culture, philosophical tradition or generation)

- **support** the claims and points that you make by picking out specific authentic examples, often from your own experience either in everyday life or in the areas that you have studied, or from media such as movies, TV, music or leisure pursuits (rather than examples others have used before you). **Check** that each example does make your point clearer

- **convince** your reader that this is your essay, and only you could have written it. Does this mean that you should use the first person ("I think")? Despite the common advice you may hear that "I" should never be used in an essay, writing in the first person can be an effective way to show that the knower's perspective in question is yours, and hence it is fine to use "I" judiciously: that is, reflecting upon your experiences critically, and balancing your perspective with consideration of different perspectives. Note, however, that using the first person is neither necessary nor sufficient for meeting this criterion.

- So, **beware** of the dangers of saying "I think": you may forget that your opinion always needs to be supported with reasons and explanations, or that you must consider what others think as well.

Criterion C looks at the quality of your analysis of knowledge issues. Analysis goes beyond merely stating or describing the KIs. You need to explore them with a high degree of depth, detail and insight. Here are some things to check.

- Whenever you make a **major claim**, you have given the reader reasons to agree with you.

- Your **arguments** should "hang together", so that, if you claim that a conclusion follows from what you have just written, it really does.

- You have **presented** and **developed** at least some counterclaims—alternative views that count against what you have been arguing. Be careful here to make it clear to the reader whose "voice" is speaking: for example, "an opponent of this view might say …". Remember also that the point of considering counterclaims is to improve your analysis. Try to deal with them, rather than just saying that there are several views.

- Your **essay flows** well: the reader knows where you are going next and why. You signpost these transitions using words and phrases such as "furthermore", "on the other hand", "In history, however, …".

- Where appropriate, you have told the reader what follows if you are right (the **implications** of your argument) and what underlying claims have been taken for granted by you or others (the **assumptions** on which views are based).

Criterion D assesses the **organization of ideas** in your essay. Here is where working out the "design of your bag" is vital. Before you start writing you should have a detailed plan. You can make sure that your ideas fit together well much better when you are working with a condensed plan than while writing full sentences and paragraphs. At the planning stage, before writing out the essay in full, and again once it is completed, you should check that:

- you have **organized** the ideas you generated in your brainstorm

- your plan/essay **addresses**, in a focused manner, the title you have chosen

- the plan/essay as a whole remains **connected and relevant**, so that the reader can easily follow your overall argument

- you have **explanations** of the key terms you identified when you unpacked the title, and that you use them in a consistent way

- you have an adequate **introduction** (which can give a brief survey of the main line of argument followed by the steps in your plan) and **conclusion** (which should refer back to the introduction and the title)

- you have gathered, and checked the accuracy of, any **facts** and ideas that you need, and kept full records of their sources, to **reference** them properly.

Now write!

When you are happy with your plan (and you have shown the plan to your teacher, and to anyone else whose judgment you trust for advice), it is time to write the essay. Expand your plan into sentences and paragraphs, then reread and edit your essay to ensure that your writing is clear, and neither ambiguous nor merely descriptive. It's a good idea to ask someone you know, whose grasp of good writing you trust, to read the essay, and highlight for you any places where they had difficulty understanding what you were trying to say. Then work on these bits until they are clearer. This is especially important if you are not writing in your native language. You will not be penalized for linguistic errors provided your meaning is clear, so make sure it is. Check again that the flow of argument is clear, and that you have not confused it with any extras you have added in at this stage.

Make sure that you have correctly **referenced** all **factual claims** (unless they are common knowledge) and ideas you got from someone else (it is, of course, possible to have written an essay that does not need referencing). If your school uses a TOK textbook that you have referred to at any point at all

during your course, you should reference the textbook as a source. Equally, you should reference any other books, magazine articles, websites and web forums that you may have visited, if they have influenced your ideas in any way. Use a standard method of referencing (it doesn't matter which, as long as you are consistent). The bottom line here is that your reader should have enough information to find your sources.

An example of referencing a book or article:

Dombrowski, E, Rotenberg, L, & Bick, M, (2007) *Theory of Knowledge Course Companion*, Oxford: OUP, pp 23–4.

An example of referencing a website:

Garvey, J, (2009), 'The Credit Crunch makes you stupid', *http://blog.talkingphilosophy.com/?p = 767*, [posted 3 March 2009, accessed 11 March 2009].

Unpacking kits and exemplar essays with commentaries

In the section to follow, we take a close look at five exemplar titles. First, to help you understand our advice better, we provide unpacking kits: examples of how to unpack and brainstorm for each title. Studying these will take you through all the steps we have recommended you take to help you remain focused upon the essay title you choose. We emphasize that these unpacking kits are just examples. Under each heading, we raise many issues and pose many questions. A good answer would not be able to—or need to—cover all of these in sufficient depth, but would concentrate on some of them. Equally, a good essay may also address other knowledge issues and use other supporting material that we have not mentioned here. Each heading, however, covers an important element of constructing a solid essay: we advise that you use them to respond in your own way, based on your knowledge and experience.

The unpacking kits show you how to identify and start to address some relevant knowledge issues in a suitably critical manner, using a range of the essay types we identified above. However, they do not show you how to take the material identified in the unpacking and brainstorming stages, and turn it into a plan, much less a full essay. In particular, we warn you against using the unpacking kit pattern as a template for the essay: all it will do is provide an unsorted pile of useful ideas. You will need to organize them into a coherent plan.

Second, the unpacking kit for each title is followed by three complete essays, representing a spread across the mark range. Each is accompanied by three sorts of examiner comments. comments explain what features of this essay met the demands of the specified criterion and hence contributed to the award of a higher achievement level, ⊙ comments explain what features of this essay contributed to the award of a lower achievement level, and further comments in blue boxes offer more general advice to you about what you can do to show your examiner that you are meeting the requirements of the criteria. For certain titles we have also added extracts, with comments, from essays that offer a different approach to the title.

Finally, in "Appendix 1", we provide an essay-unpacking/brainstorming form based on the unpacking kits, in case you would like to use it to help you choose an actual prescribed title, and start to plan your response. Using the table is not the only way to unpack and brainstorm, of course. You may choose to do it on a computer, or blank paper. Moreover, as we have said, this form will not write your essay for you. The contents of your essay should be based upon your own ideas, studies, examples, experience and observations, and following the form will help you gather that material. Planning and writing the essay, however, is up to you. We wish you well!

After reading through the kits, try to use our advice to come up with ideas of your own, for example how would you unpack a title?

Kit 1

Evaluate the role of intuition in different areas of knowledge.

[Title 1, from November 2007/May 2008]

Essay type:

A type 1 title that focuses on a TOK-related term (intuition), asking for evaluation across AOKs (your choice).

Identify key words and phrases:

- Evaluate, role, intuition, areas of knowledge

Contestable concept:

- Intuition

What do you understand by intuition?

Is it a feeling, an instinct, an emotion, a kind of unconscious perception, a paranormal process like telepathy or something else?

Ambiguous words:

- Role

Is the title implying that intuition plays the same sort of role in all AOKs? Or should you understand the question to be asking about the differing roles of intuition?

Action term:

- Evaluate

You are being asked to make suggestions about the role (or roles) intuition has in different AOKs and to weigh up the adequacy of these suggestions. For example, is intuition essential in some AOKs, important in others, but of little relevance in some?

Assumptions in the title:

- That intuition **has a role** to play in areas of knowledge

Are you going to question whether intuition has any role to play at all or are you going to accept that it does?

If intuition does have a role in an AOK, what is the nature and the extent of this role?

- (Possibly) that there is only one type of intuition

Does the nature of intuition change in different AOKs?

Rephrase the title to check your understanding

Having thought about all the above, now is the time for you to make sure you understand the intent of the whole title. One way to do this is to try to put it in your own words. Here is one possibility.

Come to a considered and supported opinion about how people may use intuition to gain knowledge in different professions and pursuits that belong to different AOKs

This is just one way the question could be rewritten. It focuses upon the people who may use intuition, how they use it, why and the activities in which intuition may have a role for them. Your unpacking of the terms may be different from this.

Identify the knowledge issues:

The title very clearly raises the KI "What is the role of intuition in different AOKs?". However, to address this question you are very likely to encounter others, such as the following:

- What exactly is the nature of intuition?

- Are there different types or kinds of intuition?

- Does intuition enable knowledge to be gained with a degree of certainty?

- Can intuition clarify the nature of human experience and the role of subjectivity in the knowledge process?

- What is the relationship between intuition and other WOKs?

Brainstorming

Consider AOKs and WOKs

The title mentions AOKs. Does intuition have a role to play in all AOKs or only in particular AOKs? Which AOKs will you concentrate on?

What is the relationship between intuition and other WOKs?

Is intuition a WOK in its own right or is it an aspect of one of the four main WOKs?

What does the way we use language when referring to intuition reveal about the nature of intuition?

Make claims and develop perspectives using authentic examples to illustrate and support your discussion:

Provide your own **examples** of intuition at work in different AOKs.

Intuition is clearly related to how we know things and the title asks you to consider AOKs.

Try to find examples based upon your own experience or that of others. One way to compare different AOKs is by considering professions that look at similar occurrences through different AOKs—a firefighter with a combustion chemist, or a horse trainer with an artist who paints horses.

Can you give a conclusive definition of intuition or does intuition need to be identified differently in each AOK?

Analyse and argue

Provide effective **counterclaims, counter-arguments** and **counter-examples** to support them.

You may wish to provide an example of a situation where it could be claimed that intuition is a WOK used by a firefighter or a horse trainer. However, you may later wish to question this with a counterclaim that the firefighter or horse trainer is using inductive reasoning or sense perception-based knowing rather than intuition.

A counterclaim can open the way for in-depth analysis; thus you could follow your counter-argument with analysis of the possible relationship between intuition and inductive reasoning and/or knowing based on experience by means of sense perception. Does consideration of this relationship reveal differences or similarities between the arts and the sciences?

Evaluate and conclude

Does intuition have a role to play in every AOK?

Are there different types of intuition, some more relevant to certain AOKs than others?

Are some kinds on intuition more certain and reliable than others?

What is the significance of intuition to the human knowledge process?

This essay achieved 11/40, a grade D

D Although the student attempts to define intuition (direct perception, immediate apprehension), there is a lack of clarity and explanation or any attempt to explore the terms offered.

Avoid using dictionary definitions unless investigating the roots or origins of a word. Provide your own explanation of terms, if possible illustrated however briefly, by a possible context for the term.

A The student relates the KI of intuition's subjectivity to the "role" of intuition in AOKs and cites this subjectivity as a reason why it would have different "degrees of importance" depending upon the AOK.

Once you define key terms, address KIs by considering the implications of those terms and the concepts that they represent upon relevant AOK and/or WOK.

D C There is no support for the claim that "information that was based upon intuition" cannot solve a mathematical problem.

This "negative claim" is ineffective on account of a lack of in-depth exploration of any relationship between intuition and induction/deduction or mathematics. The student makes unsupported assumptions.

It is very important to fully support a "negative" knowledge claim in the same way as you should do a straightforward "positive" knowledge claim.

B The nature of the role of intuition in spiritism is asserted, but not explained in knowledge terms.

Examples should be used to clarify knowledge claims and arguments.

Intuition is direct perception of truth, fact, etc., independent of any reasoning process; it is immediate apprehension. Intuition, in my point of view, is a combination of feelings and senses that lead humans to formulate opinions about known or unknown issues. The fact that intuition is defined as a very subjective way of knowing, leads to the fact that it can have various degrees of importance in different areas of knowledge. To address these differences I will analyze the role of intuition in various areas of knowledge, such as mathematics, natural sciences, religion and literature.

Intuition does not play a very large role in the field of natural sciences and mathematics. These mentioned areas of knowledge base their truth upon forensic proof and therefore require more than intuition to lead individuals to believe. One cannot solve a mathematical problem only by writing down information that was based upon an intuition, there is a need for calculations to show the means by which one could generate the results obtained. Sometimes, the intuition for a right answer can actually be mistaken for previous knowledge. For example, if the answer you have found for a Physics problem shows that the gravity of the moon is bigger than 10 ms^{-2}, one may have an intuition that the answer is wrong. This is most likely to be your previous knowledge, a remembrance that the gravity of the moon is not bigger than the gravity of the Earth. Also, concerning mathematics, intuition cannot play a major role due to the fact that ways to know can be deductive and inductive. Both these ways consist of proving your results. In deduction, one is more inclined to the use of logic while inductions consist of trial and error that will eventually lead you to an answer. Neither way has a strong intuitive factor.

Intuition can also have different roles among the religions of the world. In the religion I believe in, Spiritism, intuition plays an important role. Spiritism is a Christian religion that has its basis on the belief of resurrection, spirits and that we, human beings, are in this life to learn and develop our souls. This development is long, and the resurrection is a way to mantain a circle of learning, until a point when our being has developed enough to break out of this circle and join our Father on another level of existence. In Spiritism we believe that spirits are among us, for different purposes and reasons. The intuition and perception for external energies can therefore determine your own personal truth and opinion about the religion. On the other hand religions such as

The student presents what seems to be a counterclaim regarding intuition in religion, but again really provides no clarification. It is simply a personal opinion of the student's on Catholicism. It has no obvious relevance to the nature of the role of intuition and thus distracts from the main KI of the possible role of intuition in any AOK.

Any personal views expressed need to have their relevance demonstrated, eg by clarifying central concepts.

This personal example does very little to clarify the nature of intuition. Is intuition simply another form of sense perception? The example is left unexamined, other than to compare its presence in spiritism with its absence in Catholicism.

This is the strongest claim made about the nature of intuition: that it is about being able to perceive, judge and access truth in a very personal manner. However, the writer neither supports nor clarifies the claim. Any possible KIs remain unexplored.

Demonstrate the connection of your knowledge claims to the title and to relevant KIs.

It is unclear whether intuition can be a means by which authors can evaluate the effect of their writing. No consistent sense of this key term has been established.

Ensure that you provide clarification of key terms and claims you use, so they further the discussion.

This book is not referenced.

All sources must be referenced fully.

Catholicism are not as intuitive as Spiritism. Catholicism has a more strict doctrine regarding the beliefs and disbeliefs of the religion. For instance, to follow the principles of Catholicism one has to believe in the fact that the Catholic Church descends from the church created by Jesus Christ, the validity and purpose of Eucharist, and the belief in Jesus' divinity among other doctrines.

I personally believe in my senses and perceptions. I have experienced times in my life when I simply knew that my grandfather, who passed away when I was 3 years old, was in spiritual presence with me. These sensations and intuitions became a very common theme of conversations between my mother, my two sisters and I since I was a child. In other religions, such as Catholicism, intuition does not play a large role as a part of the religion. It may be present on a more personal level, as the feeling or perception that the action of going to church every Sunday is the right thing to be done, because one may feel inner peace and serenity. Intuition is not a part of the catholic religion as an institution as much it is in other religions, such as Spiritism, because Catholicism does not invite you to use your own perceptions of the surrounding world to make your own judgments or decide your own truth. Therefore, intuition plays a very important role in some religions and a not as important one in others, that may not leave as much room for questioning your own existence.

In my opinion, intuition plays a very important role in literature. Literature is a form of art, a representation of the world that surrounds us, that being an imaginary world or a real one. In literature, the author tries to convey messages through the writing. These messages don't always resemble truth or reality and therefore intuition plays a very important role for both the author and the readers. Authors can use intuition as a form to analyze their own writing and evaluate the feelings that the readers could get from it. By doing so, they are able to improve the writing.

The author Tim O'Brien for instance plays with the emotions of the readers in several situations. In his novel "The Things They Carried", O'Brien writes on events about the Vietnam War from the perspective of the soldiers involved. One of his aims in the novel is to make the readers contemplate the fact that personal truth can be created through stories that are not veridical. The author in this case makes use of

B D The literature example is personal, but vague. The student does not clarify key terms (personal truth, veridical). Is intuition about feelings and knowledge, or emotions? The section finishes with an incomplete sentence only adding to the confusion.

A The student asserts here that there are several ways intuition contributes to understanding a novel, but with no firm account of the nature of intuition, it is unclear how this would take place.

Any examples used or claims made should be accompanied by detailed analysis and explanation in order that thay clarify and explore the KIs.

D Stating in the conclusion that you have addressed part of what was required by the essay title will not compensate for the fact that you have not done so.

A D The conclusion evaluates the very subjective and broad nature of intuition, and also that it is contextual. These KIs should have been further explored during the essay rather than simply acknowledged at the end.

Ensure that the conclusion of your TOK essay successfully identifies KIs that have you have explored fully through examples and discussion in the main body of your essay.

intuition in order to better create feeling and a personal truth for the readers. He uses his own feelings and knowledge of the war to convey to the readers the emotions he chooses to.

For readers, on the other hand, intuition helps to obtain an idea of the message the author is trying to convey. Using O'Brien's "The Things They Carried" as an example, the readers are always trying to arrive at conclusions as to whether his work is a biography that includes real facts and characters or if his purpose is to make us believe in that while it is not actual facts. Intuition plays an important role in analyzing this author because it is a way to know that allows you to interpret the author beyond the level of written words. The intuition takes you to another level of interpretation, making you analyze the feelings that the writing creates in you and whether these feelings are generated by truth or by invented stories.

Throughout this essay I have been able to express my opinions on what role intuition plays in different areas of knowledge. Intuition does not play major roles in areas such as mathematics and the natural sciences. On the other hand, it can be very important in areas such as literature. Regarding religion, intuition depends on the context of the religion and its doctrine and beliefs. In certain religions, such as Spiritism, intuition plays a major role. Through intuition one can decide if they believe in the doctrines and says of Spiritism. On the other hand, religions such as Catholicism impose a more rigid set of beliefs, which people are asked to base their faith on. Intuition remains a very subjective way of knowing, simply because it is based on impression, feelings, emotions and it also depends on the context, which varies in every situation. Whether one can or cannot consider intuition as an important and defining way of knowing is a very personal choice to be made.

Word Count: 1219

Examiner report

Criterion A: (4): The student makes some very encouraging claims about the KIs raised by the title, such as that a central KI regarding intuition is a "subjective" means of attaining knowledge or that intuition is about being able to perceive, judge and access truth in a very "personal" manner. However, through most of the essay these views on intuition, and KIs related to it, are not clarified and neither are they supported. There are even interesting and relevant KIs that are brought into the conclusion, where they can only be mentioned, not examined or explored in any way. Therefore, in general, KIs are identified, but they are not adequately addressed or treated.

Criterion B: (3): The student provides several examples and also does mention perspectives (spiritism); however, very little explanation is provided and, indeed, the discussion is sometimes confusing so obscures rather than clarifies the relevance of the example. The student often provides insufficient clarification of *how* the examples (the novel *The Things They Carried*) clarify and support the KIs that have been identified. Far more

explanation and justification should be provided for the claim that intuition is found in religion.

Criterion C: (2): Unfortunately, the quality of analysis is such that it can be noted in terms of how little there is. The student tends to develop the essay in a very descriptive manner. It has already been noted that, regarding KIs, there are few attempts to justify the points made regarding them. There are also many unsupported assumptions made (intuition present in spiritism, the lack of intuition in mathematics). The student provides almost no counterclaims to balance the claims made, thus contributing to the lack of critical analysis.

Criterion D: (2): Although the essay is fairly well organized in terms of structure, the discussion that the student develops is often irrelevant either to the points made (intuition is not found in mathematics, it is found in religion) or to the KIs highlighted in the title. It is not always easy to follow the discussion the student provides or to understand what the student intends by making certain points (intuition is subjective) or by giving particular

examples (spiritism). Finally, the student provides only very partial referencing, so does not fully acknowledge ideas and sources of information.

Overall …

Although the essay does make some initial points that seem to address the title, the ensuing discussion of KIs, through examples such as spiritism and contexts such as religious belief and practice, is too inadequate in terms of the clarity, depth and breadth of the inquiry in order to be considered as adequate treatment of KIs implied by the title. How do you think the student could more fully support the qualities and connections claimed for intuition? Could the student have given better examples and a more adequate explanation? The low marks gained by this essay show that examples and perspectives given should be fully clarified and supported in order to develop a genuine critical inquiry that addresses the KIs.

This extract was taken from an essay that achieved 16/40, a grade D (A = 4, B = 4, C = 3, D = 5)

The student refers to historians' use of educated and natural intuition, but does not clarify or explain how or why this would involve intuition. Apart from a brief mention of primary and secondary resources, there is insufficient treatment of the historian's approach and methodologies.

When considering how knowledge tools are used in any particular AOK, explore in detail, referring to the common methods of the discipline.

History seeks to study and explain the significant events of the past on the basis of currently existing evidence. Although History is based, in part on primary sources, they are interpreted from a limited point of view. It is impossible to achieve a completely objective view of the past. Natural intuition would play a bigger part compared to educated intuition in History. Historians would probably use their educated intuition in order to do their work efficiently. But in terms of the understanding of the past itself, from the limited primary and not completely reliable secondary sources, historians would attempt to use their natural intuition to interpret the past. However, this interpretation cannot be deemed as a complete certainty. As an example, how would you interpret an ancient situation of a culture: the woman was sitting

B D The example is plausible, shows an individual approach, and is used effectively. But is it real? If so, where and when? This should be referenced. If not, then its hypothetical nature undermines the argument.

Provide relevant detailed information when developing an example. Vagueness and generalization do not help the development of meaningful discussion in an essay.

C The jigsaw puzzle comparison is too vague to clarify the differences between "educated" and "natural" intuition.

Examples must contribute to the analysis.

down on the ground and the man was sitting down on a higher ground. With most current intuition, most people would say that women were of a lower social class. Where in the *actual* scenario, women were regarded as a higher social being; therefore they were seated on the ground, closer to mother earth. It can be inferred that, intuition needs adequate information, to be utilised. Intuition is like solving a jigsaw puzzle; educated intuition would be a puzzle with complete pieces, able to be solved. On the other hand, the natural intuition would be a solved puzzle with missing pieces—the flaw and the unreliability it holds.

! **This essay achieved 21/40, a grade C**

D C The student does not support or clarify the first claim. How is intuition about "getting information without relying on the senses or reasoning"? No clear counterclaim is provided.

Explain the claims that you make as a way of supporting them (D)! Could you argue that there are strong counterclaims to the statement (C)? Try arguing against your initial claim to provide a counterclaim.

D C The student clarifies the AOK that the essay proposes to look at (D). However, they offer their opinion in the form of a conclusion about intuition, but does not support or justify their claim (C).

Intuition has many different meanings but the most accepted one is that it is getting information without relying on the senses or reasoning. In my opinion it is impossible to strictly determine whether intuition has a specific meaning in all the areas of knowledge or if it has no importance whatsoever, because certain areas of knowledge are very different and emphasize different ways of obtaining information in different ways. If we take the examples of music, math and history and apply different examples to these areas of knowledge we can see that intuition plays a certain role in all areas of knowledge, but it also varies from area to area.

Mathematics is usually perceived as an area of knowledge based on strict reasoning and has nothing to do with intuition. This makes perfect sense if we take the example of Pythagoras theorem; the way that Pythagoras got to this theorem was through reasoning, already existing mathematical theory and endless calculations. Most of us know that $c^2 = a^2 + b^2$ and we would all agree that intuition has nothing to do with this theorem. It doesn't matter if 2 people have different opinions on what the value of c is going to be for the same values of a and b, it doesn't matter if the first person thinks or "feels" that the solution is going to be greater then what the second person is expecting it to be, in each case the result is going to be the same and it won't be the affected by the intuitive opinions of the 2 people.

A good example of a counterclaim here, which the student explores and evaluates to some extent. The student also considers intuition in mathematics AOK and the example furthers the inquiry into the nature of intuition.

Relevant counter-examples can provide excellent evidence for counterclaims. They can also allow you to further develop your inquiry into the KI(s).

The student makes an unsupported assumption that historians' work is mainly about using primary sources to support theory. Surely historians still have to evaluate such information? The student shows little awareness of problems historians will have in dealing with the past.

It is important to develop a critical inquiry (C). In the case of historians, surely they need to explain events by looking at causes and other issues relating to the relevant time and place? (A).

The student gives a real-life example from current affairs. It illustrates and supports the counterclaim and the knower's opinion (perspective) above in the same paragraph.

Of course, if we look at the role of intuition in math in this way most of us will say that they have no connection whatsoever but there's always the other side: How did Pythagoras come to this conclusion that $c^2 = a^2 + b^2$? Yes, he did use mathematical theories and calculations that have already existed in order to get to the final form of the theorem as we know it today but there was something that made Pythagoras think that there is a certain relationship between sides of a triangle, there was something that made him think that the solution might be right. One may say he relied upon reasoning, using his previous knowledge but there was a point where he thought the solution might be right although he had no empirical evidence, and that was the point in time where intuition took the place of reasoning and because of which he tried to prove his theory. Of course it is impossible to apply this example to all existing theories in mathematics but this example proves that intuition has some importance in this area of knowledge.

When talking about history one may say that intuition has an important role in that area of knowledge but in my opinion history is not so closely related to intuition. We can say that history studies events that occurred sometime in the past in order to known more about our present and to predict what may happen in the future. What does that tell us about the connection between history and intuition? Well, many people would say that trying to understand the future by studying the past is so dependent on the use of intuition. If we take the example of the situation in the Middle East we can say that experts can predict what may happen using the knowledge of previous events that occurred in that area, or in some other part of the world in a similar situation. So what they are actually doing is using history to predict what is going to happen. One may say that this has many things to do with intuition, but in my opinion it has almost nothing to do with intuition, because the "experts" are not using intuition as their primary source of information. They are basing their decision on their previous knowledge of that issue and predicting that thing that can happen is going to happen only because it has occurred sometime before in history. Intuition is only used to the extent that something completely unpredictable can happen but in that case many other areas of knowledge would be affected and the principles of those areas would be broken. So when an expert says that Israelis and Palestinians are going to continue fighting he's basing his statement on the fact that they have been fighting for the last 60 years and that nothing has changed enough that we can assume that something unexpected is going to happen. Using intuition in history would be assuming that something unexpected is going to happen and not having a solid proof for it.

C

The first example is unclear in terms of developing discussion. The following counter-example does not address where intuition stands in relation to "such rules" apart from a vague implication that intuition lies "outside the rules".

Try to use examples and counter-examples in a structured and detailed manner, to address and develop inquiry into central KIs.

D

The example is not effective because it lacks clarity. The phrase "different areas of knowledge" does not seem to refer to TOK AOKs, and there is also an implication that emotion is an AOK. Or is the claim that intuition is an emotion?

Explain and carefully develop your examples. Use TOK terms accurately.

A

This statement is too generalized and vague about KIs and how they relate to AOKs and WOKs. Although it states that the role of intuition may vary between AOKs, it is unclear, speaking about "a certain role".

It is essential that you should express your discussion and arguments regarding main claims and KIs in your essay clearly.

D

There are no references for any sources used. Several factual claims (Pythagoras, Cage) need references.

Include in your bibliography any background reading you have done, such as a course textbook, plus sources for factual claims (unless they are general knowledge).

If we take the example of the arts, or specifically music, one may say that music relies upon intuition because a musical piece depends only on the composers feeling what may sound nice and what may fit in the composition. The part of music making that most people forget about are the rules of composing, so when we listen to a piece of music we may think it is only the composers intuition that played a role in arranging all those tones in a certain way that makes the composition nice to listen to, but in fact a greater role was played by all the rules of composition than the composers intuition. There are certain composers that don't follow the rules of composition and compose pieces that are very different from what we are used to. John Cage for example, one of the most prominent composers of contemporary classical music wrote a piece of music that had no actual music in it, no tones, no instruments sounding but it had one instrument which was piano. Anyone who performs that piece is supposed to sit at the piano and stay still for 4 minutes and 33 seconds. This is an example of a piece that seems to break all the rules of composing but at the same time has so many fundamental music principals involved in it. Most of the composers stick to certain guidelines when making a piece of music. That doesn't mean that intuition has no importance in actual composing, on the contrary, intuition plays the most important role in music, whether performing or composing but what also matters and is the often neglected set of rules that most composers use. If a composer makes music by following those rules it doesn't mean that he is being less imaginative or less intuitive, it only increases the beauty of his composition because he is able to make something sound beautiful by following certain guidelines but still sticks to what he thinks is soothing to the listener. When I compose a piece of music myself, I try to follow as many rules as possible but if I think a certain chord would fit my piece perfectly I will include it in the piece although it "breaks" rules of composition, but I know that different areas of knowledge are being a part of this piece so I rely on my emotions too. As a musician I know that most of the people that create music work in a similar way.

By looking at all these examples we can say that intuition may seem like something completely unrelated to some areas of knowledge but if we try to take a different perspective we will see that intuition plays a certain role in many areas of knowledge. Of course, there are areas of knowledge that are less affected by intuition, as showed on the example of history as an area of knowledge but at the same time there are certain areas that depend on intuition and overall we can say that to some extent intuition is closely related to most of the areas of knowledge.

Examiner report

Criterion A: (5): The essay demonstrates some understanding of KIs relevant to the title. Although it does not clearly establish a role or a lack of it for intuition in the AOKs, it does highlight many knowledge processes that could be mistaken for intuition. Questions are raised about the nature of intuition—is it emotion or is it related to previous experience?

Criterion B: (6): Some interesting examples show the student's perspective concerning controversy as being related to breaking conventions (Israeli–Palestinian conflict or John Cage's 4'33"); however, the relationship between intuition and controversy is not clarified. The examples are only effective in indicating the ambiguous nature of intuition. There is some evidence of the student's self-awareness as a knower ("we listen to the music" and "I think a certain chord would fit").

Criterion C: (5): The quality of inquiry into the KIs is only just satisfactory. Some counterclaims contribute to the critical

approach and tone of the essay's inquiry. Some allow examination to some degree in detail of the nature of intuition. However there are counterclaims that do not really "work" (the John Cage example), opportunities for counterclaims are missed and some points remain unjustified. In the history example (Israeli–Palestinian conflict), the student makes sweeping and unsupported assumptions about the nature of a historian's work.

Criterion D: (5): The structure of the essay is satisfactory, although it is sometimes difficult to understand what the writer intends. Although the discussion is quite well developed, some examples are not used effectively. Others seem to be irrelevant to the point being made or the student does not make clear the claim that they are supporting. The student sometimes provides firm opinions without supporting them, as in the introduction where the student indicates likely conclusions that he will reach without supporting these views. There is no attempt to reference formally the

sources used. You should not assume that naming works and authors in the essay's text satisfies the requirement to reference sources.

Overall …
Although the essay is satisfactory and addresses some interesting and partly relevant ideas, it tends to provide the student's opinions without sufficient support. There is a lack of clarity about what is meant by intuition, and vagueness about the subject areas. The student also sometimes avoids treating the KI raised in the title of the role of intuition in AOKs. Owing to some poor organization of ideas, discussion is not always sufficiently clear or coherent, which detracts from the quality of the essay's inquiry into the central KI. Some of the examples provided are very interesting; however, opportunities for exploring their implications are lost. What examples could you provide of intuition's role in AOKs and how would you explain and support them?

This essay achieved 39/40, a grade A

A The introduction raises important TOK questions for evaluating the worth of knowledge claims, such as reliability, truthfulness and validity. The student focuses on justification as a key KI.

B Two examples are offered to clarify the claim that some of our knowledge is easily and uncritically accepted. That one is correct and the other not, neatly makes a further point.

Well-chosen brief examples can show personal reflection while advancing the argument.

From the moment we are born we learn about life through our acquisition of knowledge. At first we make knowledge claims based on experience through our senses but as we grow, we begin to recognise that knowledge can come in many forms and from many different sources. Then, questions may arise in our minds about the reliability, truthfulness, nature and validity of that information of which we absorb. Among these questions may be those such as, how are knowledge claims justified? Are the following types of justification all equally reliable: sense perception, evidence, reasoning, memory, authority, group consensus, divine revelation and intuition? As we learn as individuals, we also begin to recognise that different areas of knowledge impact us in diverse ways; some we absorb more easily and are likely to accept at face value—just as we did when our parents told us that to walk near the road could be dangerous or that

Father Christmas would bring us presents if we behaved. On the scale of knowledge claims, most people rank intuition low as a form of justification. My thesis is that although it may be given less credence than other justifications for knowledge claims, it still can have a role to play and that much of what we often refer to as intuition, is also knowledge based on experience of the world or of a particular discipline. I shall need to explore the knowledge issues that come out of that claim too, in order to evaluate the role of intuition itself in different areas of knowledge (AOK).

At the heart of this question lies the concept of intuition itself. Just as the TOK 'wheel' suggests that there are four principal ways of knowing (WOK), there are people who acknowledge that there are by no means exclusive. Amongst the WOKs is perception, and in the senses, some would claim that there is also a sixth sense, often referred to as intuition. We may loosely understand intuition as the ability to know valid solutions to problems and the ability to help in decision-making. It could be interpreted as a flash of creative insight: the "eureka" moment. An academic of mental health, Dr. Paul MacLean has said that "It is what your brain knows how to do when you leave it alone." But I would argue that a brain that is 'left alone', cannot necessarily make a sophisticated knowledge claim unless it has acquired some experience of the world. Intuition plays a part in everyday activities in different levels. Although a commonly held belief that intuition is more prevalent in women, we can all make intuitive guesses to a problem presented to us regardless of gender. But what role can intuition take in different areas of knowledge, and how reliable can it be?

Can the role of intuition be considered a legitimate WOK in the human sciences? Consider this knowledge claim. I can claim to know intuitively that Manchester United will retain the Premier leaguer championship in season 2007—2008. Such a claim rests not so much on intuition but on a more rationale assessment of the statistics of the football league, the performance of certain individuals in the team at present, the opponents left to play in the season, and a whole number of variables which amount in the end to little more than an educated guess. The role that intuition plays in a knowledge claim such as the one above is weakened further by the likelihood that a counter claim can be made—even based on the same knowledge by another person that another team will triumph. In that sense, there maybe too many variables to be able to state in this case, that the role of intuition in the area of human sciences can be reliable enough at least to guarantee truth. That doesn't prevent it playing a role however, and it would be

Throughout this paragraph, real-life examples, derived from the knower's interests and experience, provide valuable opportunities for the exploration of KIs. Personal reflection shines through the balance maintained between positive and negative aspects of intuition as a way of knowing.

Use authentic examples to illustrate your knower's perspective, especially when they provide an opportunity for developing critical analysis through the assessment of claims and counterclaims.

The analysis of how intuition interacts with the WOKs sense perception and reason (again backed up with a well-chosen quote and example) adds depth to the treatment of the KI.

Explore the ways different WOKs interact—avoid either/or claims.

The sentence gives clarity and coherence by reminding the reader of the main topic of the paragraph's discussion.

This section considers the KI of intuition in the mathematics and natural sciences AOKs. The student considers mathematical experience to explore how intuition depends upon specialized experience of a discipline, implying the theory of 'educated intuition' (A).

The student then considers counterclaims in the form of a quotation and the Andrew Wiles example—strengthening the essay's critical discussion (C).

Careful use of quotations from sources and examples develops perspectives on intuition that contribute well to the discussion. (B)

almost impossible to speculate that as humans, we could avoid using intuitive thinking when we consider problems. Being fond I of horse riding, I can say that I have used intuition when taking jumps on my horse. Although my horse and I have both been trained to know how to jump and have experience of them, there is a certain level of underlying intuition each time. This intuition guides me as to how exactly I should approach the jump and guide my horse over it. This is what I meant when I referred earlier to needing knowledge about the world in order to make a more sophisticated knowledge claim. When we employ intuition, we need to ally it with reality. Lagemaat said, "Intuition isn't the enemy, but the ally, of reason." When living in Peru I saw evidence of the role of intuition through animals. There were frequent earthquakes in Lima and, seconds before the earth shook, dogs would start barking and my pet birds would screech. Perhaps dogs "felt" the ground beneath them before we could, and birds sensed the arrival of a tremor. Was this intuition allied with reason? Animals may use intuition to sense that an earthquake was coming and they were an excellent warning for my family. I believe that in the human sciences we can see the role of intuition playing a more significant role than some other areas of knowledge.

The role of intuition in the areas of knowledge of the natural sciences and mathematics is more problematic in the sense that, as scientific thinking has developed and gained prominence in western civilization with knowledge claims, then the tendency to discount and reject intuitive thinking has became more widespread in the twentieth century. As a knowledge issue, we consider the methods of verification and justification appropriate in the above areas of knowledge then intuition couldn't easily be applied to a mathematical problem. Maths involves reasoning and, if I was given a problem to solve and came up with a solution then the feeling that the answer is correct, is not good enough. There is a logical solution and my intuition may be not only misguided here but have helped me come to the wrong answer. Jonas Salk has commented, "Intuition will tell the thinking mind where to look next". Again, a brain that has insufficient knowledge or experience in a AOK is much less likely to be able to use intuition in any capacity which could come up with a reasonable knowledge claim. In 1993 an English mathematician Andrew Wiles developed a solution to a mathematical problem known as Fermat's Last theorem. He described his long attempt to find a solution as, "a journey through a dark unexplored mansion" in which he stumbled around looking in room after room and bumping into furniture until he found the light switch which illuminated the room. That could be a considered as a kind of intuition but again is based on a brain with knowledge and experience. Karl Popper thought that both scientists and artists use intuition in common in that both are "seekers after truth who make indispensable use of intuition" The role of intuition in the above areas of knowledge may be less important, but it can play a part.

What is the role of intuition in the arts? Here, people are on more comfortable ground when it comes to using intuition in knowledge claims made in the arts. Musicians and artists refer to a 'feeling' when creating or playing a piece of work that they must include a specific note or a colour of paint. Louis Armstrong, when asked about what jazz is replied, "Man, if you've gotta ask what it is, you ain't never gonna get to know" suggesting that the role of intuition is highly important in this area of knowledge. Here at school, when I spoke with an artist, she said that artists seem to use intuition in the sense that they have the instinct for where to put the brush when painting and how to blend one colour with another. Their creativity for a piece of work can come from their instinct and intuition of what to create. What some may call intuition in deciding which note to play or which colour to use is also dependent on experience and knowledge already there, used in a creative manner.

To draw some conclusions from the above discussion, what is the role of intuition in different areas of knowledge? Knowledge claims are made in every discipline and it has been suggested from the above that flashes of intuition or creativity can and have helped produce breakthroughs in ideas. A knowledge issue which has arisen concerns the justification for the common acceptance of a female intuition—and one may conclude that there is little rational basis for such a belief. But I believe intuition is and can be important when making certain decisions and that intuition does play a role. But intuitive thinking can only be really productive when it is has a base of experience and knowledge to support it. Lagemaat comments that "expert intuition is generally more reliable than natural intuition" so if one's intuitions coincide with those of others, then one may be more inclined to accept it. It has brought new knowledge to people and has consciously or subconsciously aided people in their everyday decisions. "The power of intuition will protect you from harm until the end of your days". To disregard it would be to disregard an important way of knowing. Intuition plays a significant role in life and is of high value to some people, including myself.

B A

The student introduces the nature of intuition in the arts, illustrating it through examples of terms, concepts and situations that artists (musicians) use in their work and giving examples also from the visual arts, highlighting the role that intuition is likely to have in the arts. There is discussion of the examples used to develop the KI that intuition is related to instinct and experience.

In a TOK essay that examines a knowledge concept such as intuition, truth or justification, it is wise to include examples and perspectives from a variety of AOKs, at least two, preferably three.

A D

This is a successful conclusion, which summarizes the central KIs as well as the main claims, viewpoints and counterclaims made to examine and discuss the KIs. The worth of intuition as a tool to gain knowledge is evaluated.

In your conclusion, draw together the main threads of your essay's discussion in a critical manner.

Sources of information and ideas are acknowledged. Most of the referencing permits the tracing of sources and the word limit has been met.

Bibliography

Abel, Reuben, (1984) "Man is the Measure" Free Press

Lagemaat, van der, Richard, (2005) "Theory of Knowledge for the IB Diploma" Cambridge Press

TOK Diploma Programme Guide IBO. (2006)

http://www.worldofquotes.com/author/Lao~tse/1/index.html (Feb 17th 2008)

http://www.pbs.org/wgbh/nova/proof/wiles.html (Feb 19th 2008)

http://www.worldofquotes.com/topic/Intuition/1/index.html (Feb 19th 2008)

http://www.laurienadel.comlsixth_sense.htm (Feb 19th 2008)

Personal interview with Sophie Dilley, February 11th 2008

Examiner report

Criterion A: (10): The student first addresses the KIs such as the certainty of knowledge gained through intuition. The student considers the nature and the definition of intuition before examining the central KI. To investigate the role played by intuition in AOKs referred to in the title, the student contrasts mathematics and the arts in order to explore differences between them as a context in which intuition may have a role. This motivates an in-depth inquiry into perspectives and arguments regarding the central KI concerning the nature and the extent of the role of intuition in AOKs.

Criterion B: (10): The student shapes the essay in a personal manner using real-life examples (football or horse riding), which derive from the knower's interests and experience. These show a personal engagement with the KIs as well as self-awareness as a knower. The student makes careful use of quotations from sources and examples (Andrew Wiles) in order to develop perspectives upon intuition that make a valuable contribution to the essay's discussion.

Criterion C: (9): The student makes claims that are well justified by examples, perspectives and arguments. Claims are counterbalanced by counterclaims that are then explored and evaluated (intuition a female knowledge tool versus evidence that it is used universally), which strengthens the critical aspect of the essay's discussion. The student critically analyses knowledge perspectives (intuition as based on empirical experience).

Criterion D: (10): The essay is very well organized, which makes it easy to follow the argumentation and the progress of the inquiry into the KI. The student refers to key TOK concepts (the wheel or diagram) that help clarify ideas and claims to the reader. Particular features of this essay are the devices used to introduce, recap or emphasize ideas and short discussions. These include statements and questions that introduce paragraphs and also concluding statements that summarize arguments and discussions.

Overall …

The student provides various arguments for the nature and the role of intuition and supports claims by a comprehensive use of examples, relevant quotations and well-developed consideration of the KIs within the context of various AOKs. How compelling do you find the evidence and arguments given for the roles of intuition in different AOKs? Do you agree that the student could possibly have considered more counterclaims in order to strengthen the argument? Nevertheless, generally a very competent and well-developed handling of the topic.

This extract was taken from an essay that achieved 40/40, a grade A (A = 10, B = 10, C = 10, D = 10)

The extract begins with a claim followed by a counterclaim. These are later supported by examples, including one that is examined in detail.

You will find that your essay can develop step by step if your focus is upon claims, then provide counterclaims relevant to the key KIs. Support your discussion and argumentation with authentic examples that you explore in detail.

The student shapes the essay in a personal manner by seriously considering different perspectives. Self-awareness is shown by the ability to clearly voice a personal view, whilst also offering alternatives to it.

Even seemingly everyday, anecdotal examples can be used to develop analysis through skilful use of counter-examples and alternative views.

The student develops detailed inquiry, focusing well upon a KI central to the title, that of the extent to which ethics relies most upon intuitive thinking. The student explores this through arguments for and against the claim.

By considering statements that are later rejected, as well as examples and counter-examples, the extract develops a well-sustained argument.

Argumentation should be detailed and take the form of a tennis match, with claims, counterclaims, examples and counter-examples being bounced back and forwards!

In the light of the fact that Ethics is in part determined by emotional response, most students may be tempted to argue that it is in fact the area of knowledge that relies most heavily on intuitive thinking; such reasoning, in my opinion, is far too simplistic. I believe that our moral judgements are based on elaborate processes of socialization, whereby we acquire our moral foundation through the testimonies of the main sources of authority in our lives, such as our parents, teachers, priests, imams, etc. This socialization, when combined with our emotional sensibility, allows us to be particularly in tune with detail, an acuteness which we often confuse with our intuition. My friend claims that she has an amazing intuition. When I asked her why, she replied: "*Since the very first day of school, I always had this gut feeling that Kenza didn't appreciate me, despite her claims otherwise. Last week, as I was entering Science class, I overheard her telling David that she cannot stand me!*" When I asked my friend what was the basis of this intuition, she gave me a confused look and replied: "*Uh, I don't know, the way she stared at me from head to toe?*" My friend is a perfect example of how we mistake our keenness to detail with intuition; her alleged intuition was simply specialized insight into a circumstance based upon prior experience. When a girl consistently stares at you 'from head to toe', you assume that she holds strong feelings against you. However, if my friend had never been taught that the act of staring 'from head to toe' is in fact an indication of dislike, my friend would not have 'intuitively' suspected any tension between her and Kenza.

Does language play roles of equal importance in different areas of knowledge?

[Title 4, from November 2007/May 2008]

Essay type:

A type 3 title that focuses upon a WOK (language), and requires comparison across AOKs (your choice).

Key words and phrases:

- Language, roles of equal importance, areas of knowledge

Contestable concepts:

- Language

What is the nature of language? Which of the different accounts of language will you use?

How important is language in the process of gaining knowledge?

Ambiguous terms:

- Equal

Do the roles have to be the same to be equal? Or can they be different but just as significant?

Action terms:

- Roles of equal importance

You are being asked to come to a considered decision on the relative significance of the roles played by language in at least two AOKs. This will first require you to identify and clarify the role or roles.

Assumptions in the title

- That language plays a role.

- That language plays a role in every AOK.

Can you question whether language plays any role at all in some particular AOKs?

- That we can measure and compare the importance of role.

Is importance something we can compare, measure or weigh up, especially when the roles might be different?

Rephrase the title to check your understanding

Try to do this by rephrasing the title into your own words. A possibility could be:

- Make a judgment about the relative significance of language as a medium for acquiring or for manipulating knowledge in several diverse disciplines and contexts.

There are other ways in which the title could be rephrased. This one focuses upon the nature and value of language as a medium for knowledge acquisition. Your unpacking of the terms may be different from this.

Identify the knowledge issues

The title very clearly raises the KI "Does the importance and the nature of the role of language vary from one AOK to another?". However, to address this question you are very likely to encounter others, such as the following:

- To what extent can language manipulate knowledge?

- Do issues of interpretation and ambiguity arise to the same degree in all AOKs?

- To what extent might each AOK be seen as having its own disciplinary or professional specialist language? Does this give rise to the issue of language as understandable only in context, or issues such as exclusion of the layperson through jargon?

- Could we know anything if we had no language at all? Are some types of knowing independent of language?

Brainstorming

Consider WOKs and AOKs

This title focuses on language; so it is important to explore the nature and features of language as a WOK.

How does language allow knowledge to be gained? Or are there characteristics of language that hinder knowledge acquisition? Can you evaluate language as a tool to gain knowledge?

To what extent is language an independent WOK—or is it always used in interaction with one or more of the other WOKs?

To what extent does the language used create specialist or professional communities?

Since this title does not specifically mention any of the AOKs, you will have to decide which ones (least two, probably three) you will consider and compare in your answer.

To give yourself opportunities to compare, it is helpful to use contexts that allow you to contrast AOKs and the roles played by language as a WOK in them.

Consider WOKs and AOKs

To what extent are symbolic systems, such as mathematical, musical, or computer notations, like or different from languages?

Make claims and develop perspectives using authentic examples to illustrate and support your discussion

Obviously you use language on a daily basis, but try to **use examples** that **raise** or **support** issues that you discuss in your essay.

You may wish to claim that language plays a more important role in history than in mathematics; or, in the arts, language plays a more important role in literature than in music. Draw on your own studies for significant examples.

Language can play a role in different types of arts or media, be it a scientific journal, a painting, a piece of music or a movie website. How does language define the communities in which artists or scientists take part?

How can language influence political perceptions and ethical decisions?

Analyse and argue

Provide effective counterclaims, counter-arguments and counter-examples to support them.

However, you may want to counter the above claims by arguing and demonstrating through examples, that mathematics and/or music are forms of language. You would need to provide perspectives and examples to support this counter-argument.

How can language reveal underlying social and cultural issues? Multilingual situations may raise cultural and translation issues, such as the dialogue in the school playground in an international school, or in other formal or informal contexts.

It has been argued that, owing to its rule-governed yet open-ended and creative nature, language demonstrates the contextual nature of knowledge. Do you agree that the meaning conveyed by language can be fully understood only in context?

Evaluate and conclude

Make final comments on the significance of language to human knowledge process.

Can it be concluded that in some AOKs language is the most fundamental vehicle or medium for gaining, communicating or sharing knowledge? And that it plays a minor role in others?

If language has a wider definition that includes any art, mathematical or scientific terms, codes, scripts or symbols, can it be argued that it is the most fundamental WOK?

This essay achieved 14/40, a grade D

B

Using hypothetical and extreme examples or situations like this one is not helpful. In an introduction, it is rarely helpful to introduce situations that are by definition implausible or impossible.

Avoid using hypothetical examples and situations. An authentic example presents many opportunities for analysis due to the possibility of realistically applying perspectives according to different knowers' contexts.

A

The claim that the AOKs are all forms of language is a KI that could very usefully be argued, but cannot be assumed. This is a controversial KI that needs to be supported with examples and perspectives.

If you find yourself making a major claim, decide whether the claim is worth debating. If it is, this indicates that it is a KI that can be analysed through making claims and counterclaims, well supported by appropriate examples.

Imagine being in a world where each person had their own language and had their own unique way to communicate. Also imagine making art, making music, and creating things that no one else could understand. Not only would humans question their existence, but they would most likely cease to exist. There would be absolutely no point in discovering something like the telephone and having no use for it. Art would not be art, music would not be music, math would not be math, science would not be science, and humans would not be humans. Areas of Knowledge are also crucial because the ways of knowing (which includes language) are elements that enhance the areas of knowledge. This includes:

Mathematics, Natural Sciences, Human Sciences, History, The Arts, and Ethics. Communication, especially in the 21st Century, has become such a crucial part of our lives. We use it to express ourselves, to understand others, but most importantly it is used to enhance our areas of knowledge.

Before we answer the question about the roles of language in the areas of knowledge, we must first understand the importance of language by itself. Language can be defined as a common group of meanings used to communicate information. Language is also defined as a tool or a way of knowing for the different areas of knowledge. So what exactly is language then? Yes language is English, French, Italian, Hindi, etc. But it also goes deeper than that. Like mentioned earlier language is a common group of meanings, therefore art, music, math, science, gestures, movements, etc. are all some form of language. Languages used everyday by normal people (like English, French, etc) is the most common way language is used. If a person walked up to you and asked you "Hello, how are you?" you would most likely respond, "Fine, Thank you" On the other hand if a person walked up

B

This example is personal, but it is not doing much to support the argument, as it is used in a trivial, even flippant manner. Furthermore, it contains the dubious assumption that inhabitants of a village would not speak several languages.

D

The student has not referenced the source of this quotation.

All quotations, citations and factual information should be referenced using a standard method.

B

Although this personal example is an authentic one based upon the writer's experience, they do not connect it to wider viewpoints upon the KI of the role of language in AOKs. It would be interesting to discuss the difference between English used in Bangladesh and native speaker English used in the US; also, the role of culture in learning.

Ensure that any example you use is related to at least one or more perspectives upon the KI. These viewpoints should be linked to sources and/or to AOK or WOK.

A C

Although the claim that mathematics uses universally shared symbols and notation is worthwhile (A), it should be clarified, supported and analysed in more depth (C).

Clarify and support claims. Use authentic, more complex rather than hypothetical, simplistic examples. Consider possible counterclaims or counter-examples.

to you and said "Kemon Achen?" what would you say? To understand what this person was asking, we must have some understanding of their language. Therefore we can conclude: It is very simple to communicate information among each other, as long as they are within the same language. There are always many cases of where one person knows more than one language. My sister, one of the smartest people I know, has learned over five languages in different countries. Obviously communication for her is much easier than a person who has grown up in a village in the corner of the earth. So if you are planning a trip abroad, feel free to contact my sister because she will most likely be able to translate for you. As you can tell, language by itself has such a great role and therefore it must have some sort of contribution in the different areas of knowledge.

Earlier, we mentioned that language was a way of knowing and it is only ONE of the four tools needed for the areas of knowledge. The other three are: emotion, reason and sense perception. Even though these are very crucial, Rita Mae Brown describes the power of language perfectly: "Language exerts a hidden power, like a moon on the tides." This quote by Rita Brown is very fitting because language's power is hidden, yet so overwhelming. When I was in 6th Grade, I lived a small country known as Bangladesh. Half way through the year, my parents told me that we were going to move to the United States. This may not seem like a significant event to most people, but the move to America crippled one, and the most important, way of knowing. Even though I knew some English when I moved, the barrier that the different language caused was simply overwhelming. Switching a language and attempting to adapt to it immediately is one of the most difficult tasks. I remember sitting in my English class, understanding every other word and trying to piece together sentences. Communication became such a large problem and worst of my entire crippled tool cut off any way to enhance my areas of knowledge. Language had a crucial role in almost all of the Areas of Knowledge. Not only would I sit in class and not understand a word teacher would say, but I also would be at home struggling to do homework. After a lot of hard work, I finally picked up the commonly used language, English, which in turn helped repair my crippled "tool".

While I was adapting to move from Bangladesh to America, I noticed that one area of knowledge was not as affected as the others. This area of knowledge was Mathematics. Mathematics itself has a language of its own, and this language is universal. Now you might say that there must be other variables involved for this to be true. However no matter what variable is thrown in, Mathematics has and always will have a language of its owm. X times Y equals XY and 2 plus 2 equals 4 has the same meaning in the United States, in France, in China and in every corner of the world. A good example of this situation would be to study a foreign exchange student. Here is a hypothetical situation: A girl from Germany comes to the United States, and she has never spoken a word in English. If this student's grades are to be studied and contrasted to her grades in Germany, there will be some striking results. You will most likely see a steep decline in all her subjects EXCEPT for Mathematics. Her grades in math will have some kind of consistency in them because once again math is a universal friendly subject.

On a contrasting side, Art is an interesting subject to study for the importance of language. Even though it isn't as drastic and powerful as the other ones, it still has some striking yet subtle importance. Art requires the understanding of so many different concepts and skills. It also has a plethora of media that can be investigated and every single different medium has a language of its own. An artist must know what and how to shade, color and all the other concepts involved in art. Some say that only an artist can truly admire a piece of art. This statement is mostly true, with a few flaws. It is true that an artist CAN admire a piece of art because they have more knowledge about the medium, the color, and the shades. However, a person with no artistic eye can also admire the piece of art and it connects with a person. However, the artist and the other person have completely different viewpoints. This is a very similar situation in music as well. Even though it is a subtle language, a good grasp of the concepts is crucial. For a musician to pick up a piece of music, he/she must have a good knowledge about notes. tone, pitch, etc. Just like in art, a musician can admire the music as much as a person with no musical ear at all. However, the admirations have a completely different meaning. One might THINK the song/ artwork is about love, while the person with musical/artistic talent KNOWS it is about hate.

As you can see, language is a crucial part of our daily lives. We use it to express love, hate, and anger, communicate discoveries, hide discoveries and we simply use it almost every second. Language is one of, if not the MOST important tool needed to enhance persons Areas of Knowledge. Once again as Rita Brown once said "Language exerts hidden power, like the moon on the tides" could not be truer. The hidden powers that language holds not only play a role of equal importance in the knowledge areas, but it is the MOST crucial tool in the Ways of Knowing.

The introductory statements to this paragraph clarify the central topic, which is the role of language in the arts.

Introduce each new area to your TOK essay in a new paragraph and with very clear statements that indicate the central KI to be discussed.

The inquiry in this section is the closest to "satisfactory" in the essay. However, it falls short in terms of argumentation, which is based upon examples, claims and counterclaims that are too hypothetical to allow serious exploration of any KIs.

The student has not justified the concluding claim that language is "crucial". He has not effectively explored the KI concerning the role of language in the AOKs. The student simply decides language does have an important role to play in the AOKs by developing the tautological argument that, since we communicate through language, then language must be "crucial".

Achieve quality in your essay's inquiry into a KI by considering a counterclaim to every claim you make. Compare different AOK as contexts for your claims.

Examiner report

Criterion A: (3) The essay provides only some superficial treatment of KIs owing to a failure to define satisfactorily and develop key concepts implied by the terms in the title. Even the central term, language, is itself only explained in a tautological manner that does not allow any KIs to be seriously addressed.

Criterion B: (4) Although the essay attempts some personal engagement, this is generally done through inappropriately extreme and hypothetical examples. Consequently there is little in the way of opportunity to explore different perspectives. An authentic example of an experience of learning problems after a move to the US from Bangladesh is insufficiently connected to relevant perspectives and KIs.

Criterion C: (3) The main problem with the quality of analysis is the ineffective attempt to justify the main points with mostly inappropriate examples. Counterclaims given are equally inappropriate and the overall inquiry too anecdotal and hypothetical to allow for coherent inquiry.

Criterion D: (4) Although the essay is written quite well in terms of expression, such as some clear introductory sentences to paragraphs, the actual ideas are often incoherent. Arguments are also ineffective because of a lack of valid or factual support. There is no acknowledgment of sources such as the Brown quote.

Overall …

This essay shows how, when there is a failure to address satisfactorily any of the assessment criteria, the connections between the four criteria become evident. In an unsatisfactory essay such as this one, an inadequate response in terms of one criterion often leads to a failure to satisfy another, for example, inadequate claims and discussion regarding KIs (A) relevant to the title often lead to an equally unsatisfactory quality of analysis (C).

How could the student have shown that he understood and appreciated the central KIs in relation to the title right from the start? How could he better explore the KIs through authentic examples? What relevant perspectives might you have come across through your reading and research? How can you ensure that you balance claims with counterclaims and make sure that you clarify and explain all the terms you use?

This essay achieved 20/40, a grade C

The student does not provide the essay title as published in the prescribed title list. The modified title leads them astray. Despite the claim in the introduction that the roles are equal, the student merely discusses some roles that language plays in different AOKs, without considering the relative importance of those roles.

Always include the prescribed title to achieve greater clarity, and to be able to refer to the title in order to ensure that the essay responds to it.

The student does not tell us how "language" is going to be understood in this essay. The introduction implies language is just a means of transmitting thoughts. The lack of a clear understanding of what counts as language recurs throughout the essay.

An introduction should explicitly clarify key terms, and tell the reader how the title will be addressed.

Language: A way of Knowing

In the different areas of knowledge, language plays a very important role as it is a way to decipher our thoughts. Knowledge depends on human thoughts and these in turn depend on language to be transmitted and to become understood. As a result, language has become equally important in vast areas of knowledge.

We encode and create various symbols to correlate with the environment we live in. When a person moves from one society to another, the mechanisms of communication are dissimilar as people can decipher it in numerous ways. When one starts learning a different language or moves to another country, they may initially experience a state of confusion. This forms a barrier between what you can learn from another society and what you can share with them about your cultural background. While there is often a misconception of language that only relates to the dialect we use to share ideas between people,

D C

"While there is often a misconception" implies this is intended to be a counterclaim, but the rest of the sentence is quite unclear (D). Without analysis or examples to illustrate, clarify and support the claim (C), there is no way of resolving the many ambiguities in this statement. Several terms (dialect, symbols, fixed behaviours) are not clarified.

Quality of analysis (C) requires organization and clarity of ideas (D). Support claims with explanation and/or examples to provide clarification.

B

This is an effective example, which illustrates and supports the claims the student makes. It is an original example that very likely comes from the student's studies or interests. It therefore furthers the "Knower's Perspective" by demonstrating an awareness of the issue of bias in history and the role of language in this process.

Provide authentic examples deriving from your studies or interests.

B

The claim concerns history as an AOK; however, the example the student gives to illustrate this issue is taken from a novel—that is, fictitious literature—and therefore concerns the arts rather than history.

It is important to provide examples that come from the same AOK as the claim. That way, the examples can demonstrate that the KI being treated is relevant to the AOK being discussed.

symbols and fixed behaviors are used as well to make sense in the large spectrum of comprehension.

The language used in mathematics is said to be universal, as the symbols used in it are fairly common throughout the world. Mathematics isn't functional though unless it is a substitution from things regularly found in our surroundings. What are the advantages for knowing that 1 +2 = 3? The numbers should represent things found across the world such as: money, shapes, programs, or apples. In a math class, we are expected to solve word problems as a translation exercise to make a subconscious realization that mathematics can be found and utilized everywhere. Thus, mathematics would not be important if it was not a form of language.

The base of history is language. The way history is told is significant and any variations can sometimes make interpretations problematic. In the United States, the fact that Texas obtained its independence from Mexico is told and taught as a glorious occasion; while in Mexico this same event is remembered as a failure from Santa Anna that lead to the loss of precious land. While that case was applied to show the obvious discordance between two countries, there have been times in which other countries have agreed upon their versions of past events. For example, the nuclear bombs dropped on Hiroshima and Nagasaki is seen as a negative incident by both the United States and Japan. Renditions from two or more existing languages show the importance of words for the perception and gaining of information. The Bible can often be misread when there is a lack of knowledge about the dialogue and idioms it originated from. In addition, history can also be changed using language. In *1984*, the protagonist's job was to change history through the use of Newspeak, the language adopted by the party who in this case controls everything. "Winston's greatest pleasure was his work. Most of it was a tedious routine, but included in it there were also jobs so difficult and intricate that you could loose yourself in them as in the depths of a mathematical problem—delicate pieces of forgery in which you had nothing to guide you except your knowledge of the principles of Ingsoc and your estimate of what the party wanted you to say." (Orwell, George 49) In fictional writings usually when a form of government takes control over a population, manipulating the language becomes a matter of great importance. In the *Handmaid's tale* by Margaret Attwood the government prohibits any kind of writing, this enables them to have control over people's knowledge. In the formal way of gaining historic facts used today, whenever scripts are found they are broken down and analyzed for their literal and metaphorical content. Practices like these can lead to instances which can impair or tarnish history.

Ethics is often a popular subject as many hold other opinions about what is right or wrong. Some countries hold beliefs in which a man can hold many wives as long as they treat them well; others find this as a type of infidelity and consider it immoral. The definition of adultery becomes noteworthy since some wives accept this polygamous tradition because sexual intercourse is not performed outside of marriage. However, the definition of marriage is open to debate given that some believe it can only happen between a man and a woman, others between multiple spouses, and now between those of the same sex. Moreover, censorship depends on language as it is necessary to determine what exactly represents inappropriateness. While some think that Gustav Klimt's works are pornographic, others disagree b*y simply suggesting that his art is a more dramatic and aesthetically pleasing illustration of beautiful* nude women. Linguistic ethics are also an interesting subject that is up to date. In some customs, certain mannerisms are used out of respect for superior individuals or the elderly such as title names or conversation topics. When ideas like these clash between cultures it is imperative and honorable to confront the issue at hand instead of starting a fight.

Art is form of language by itself since it both exchanges emotions and ideas. While some people might find visual art just as rich as speech, it cannot be disregarded that a decent piece with a given explanation can be a rather fulfilling experience. In Spain you can go Museo Reina Sofia and appreciate Pablo Picasso's *Guernica*. Anyone is capable of detecting the instant pain, terror, oppressiveness and contrasting feelings being portrayed by the strong black, white and grey colors set as the background. One can relate it to war because of the injuries, the screams, the misery, and the broken blade. When the circumstances about the Spanish Civil War are provided, an easier recognition of the symbols can be found such as the bull and the donkey which reveal the rival native groups that were battling against each other. When a person shares their opinion about a particular field of interest, this can lead to more interesting judgments. For instance, when I was told by a tourist guide that the light bulb represented God's eye in Picasso's painting, this helped me recognize how the people within it looked with hope towards it. It more or less leaves an impression of shamefulness to the viewer by showing how embarrassing it is to let an almighty being observe such a brutal human act as war. Instruments and sounds

B A

This example is one of the essay's strengths since it provides useful illustrations and clarification of marital relationships as an ethical KI. The student highlights the KI as being related to language by indicating the relationship between language definitions and cultural norms. The student provides several terms, such as "fidelity" or "adultery", of which the definition depends upon the cultural context in which the term is used. The inclusion of (marriage) "between those of the same sex" relates the KIs to law and human sciences.

D

Unclear ideas in this section impede the essay's inquiry. It is unclear what the example of Klimt's works demonstrates. Is it the historical relativity of ideas? Is it whether it shows the ethical controversies that can be caused by the arts as an ambiguous AOK? The section lacks explanations.

Provide explanations in order to clarify examples and how they relate to the KIs under discussion. Each point made needs to be explained and illustrated and clearly related to previous claims and/or counterclaims in order to achieve depth as well as clarity.

These two statements should be separated by a paragraph break. There are other similar parts in this essay, where discussion on one topic runs straight into that on another topic, with no paragraphing to organize the ideas.

In order that an essay's argumentation develops clearly and effectively, each new topic, issue or example should be introduced in a new paragraph.

The discussion here is very superficial and needs to be further developed. Too many AOKs are included and then treated with a lack of depth and analysis. The essay does develop ethics, arts and history to some extent and would have been better focusing on these.

The concluding paragraph is difficult to understand, and introduces areas that were not developed in the essay. It makes no reference to the title.

Although there is no one correct manner in which to conclude a TOK essay, a successful conclusion reviews and evaluates the central areas from the title that were set up in the introduction and covered in the essay. You can provide your own opinion, but it must be well supported.

can also express these same sensations. The language of music and the reactions it can create and transmit is essential for composers, conductors, singers, and dancers. Song and dance are collective expressions in their own structure and are very similar when it comes to signifying its place of origin. Language can be modified to a creative value, as it can become very appealing in the form of rhyming poetry and intensive writing.

Two distinct regions of knowledge include the natural and human sciences. Natural sciences are related to discerning our environment and knowing more about the universe in general, while human sciences are about examining and clarifying personal actions. While in mathematics, the periodic table and the metric system are frequently used in the natural sciences to facilitate this scientific knowledge; language and its explanations are necessary to spread the awareness of these new discoveries. Nonetheless, human sciences are greatly tied to language because of their relation to the physical and mental understanding of words.

Language as a way of learning is very crucial as it can instruct or convey an assortment of concepts about knowledge. Without this system of visual, oral, and auditory qualities, cognitive processes could not be attained to make sensible choices or hold intellectual beliefs. Consequently, language is like a chain that is held tight by interlocking reasoning with perception that join together to form knowledge.

Bibliography

Orwell George. <u>1984</u>. United States: McDougal Littell Inc, 1998.

Word Count: 1292

Examiner report

Criterion A: (5) Although the essay remains reasonably relevant, discussing some aspects of the role of language in each AOK, it lacks depth of treatment and does not assess the relative importance of language in different AOKs. Too many AOKs are considered; the student would have done better to focus upon three, at most four.

Criterion B: (5) The art and ethics examples show an independent approach but the relatively brief considerations of each AOK do not demonstrate much personal involvement. Different approaches (for example to Klimt's art, to historical interpretations) are mentioned rather than fully explored.

Criterion C: (5) The essay explores some aspects of the role of language and briefly justifies some claims made (marriage, Guernica), though elsewhere arguments are unclear and/or incomplete (human and natural sciences, conclusion).

Criterion D: (5) There is a basic structure, around the six AOKs, but the introduction and conclusion are both weak, and the overall argument is not consistently developed. Key concepts (language) are not well explained, though their use is generally reasonably consistent. Most facts are reasonable, and some of the referencing is fine.

Overall …

The main overall issue with this essay is that it tries to cover too many issues/examples, so lacks the space (word limit!) to go into sufficient depth in many cases. It would work better to decide what job each treatment is intended to do, within the overall structure of the essay. It would then be possible to focus more on the important ones, and eliminate those that do not lead anywhere.

Receiving a C grade, the essay is by definition "satisfactory": despite the criticisms it's by no means a bad essay; however, it does needs a clearer sense of purpose.

If you were advising the author of this essay, what suggestions would you give for improving? The need for a better introduction and conclusion has already been highlighted. How could these and also a better quality of inquiry be achieved?

This essay achieved 37/40, a grade A

D

In the introduction, the student clearly sets out the areas to be covered, and also indicates the nature of the response to the central KI.

Use the introduction to provide an overview of your essay and to provide clarity regarding the central KIs as well as an indication of your response to the KIs.

A

The early clarification and evaluation of the KIs related to the title is very helpful. The student does this while highlighting the strong links between ethics and language and assessing the role of emotion.

Introduce each new section of your essay with a paragraph that clearly sets out and addresses the KIs and related TOK concepts such as WOKs or AOKs.

Language, emotion, reason and perception, are ways of knowing. Language is critical for knowers as it enables them to express and pass on their knowledge for the benefit of future generations. However, I believe that language plays an unequal role of importance in the six areas of knowledge. I believe, and will demonstrate through examples from the areas of ethics, natural sciences and the arts, that language has the greatest role to play in ethics followed by the natural sciences. I believe that, of the three I have cited, the arts use language, as opposed to the other ways of knowing, the least.

Ethics, which deals with the values relating to human conduct with respect to the rightness and wrongness of certain actions, uses language as an integral component of knowing. It also uses emotion to a large degree but I believe that it is language which generates the emotion which, in turn, will be used in making an ethical decision. Over the years, issues such as abortion and euthanasia have been debated by politicians and human rights protesters. Admittedly, discussing such issues can generate emotional distress which helps to educate knowers about the topic in question. However, language is employed by skilled orators in order to spin and persuade and, in doing so, cause this grief. As a debater myself, I have frequently used specific vocabulary in order to instigate emotion and educate an audience with regards to an ethical issue. Perhaps it is these personal experiences which have led me to my belief that language plays such an important role in ethics as I have experienced and utilised its power firsthand. This tactic of using language to one's advantage is visible on most ethical campaign group websites. *Pro-choice*, a pro-abortion lobby group, has a question posed boldly on its homepage: "Will parenthood ruin your life?" Clearly they are drawing attention to some of the myths spread by anti-abortionists which claim that by having an abortion a mother's life would be forever *ruined*. The verb 'to ruin' is both strong and harsh and the statement makes no reference to the many joys of parenting. This is done so that a casual reader might click on the link, believing it to be anti-abortionist when in fact the page which loads explains that parenthood is one of the greatest joys in life. Likewise, Pro-choice refers to "Post-Abortion Syndrome" as being a "myth generated by anti-abortion proponents which has not been recognised scientifically or medically". By dismissing one of the greatest concerns many women feel when deciding whether to have an abortion as a "myth", Pro-choice is successfully using language in order to educate others by their own values.

Pro-life uses language on their website in order to persuade readers that abortion is wrong. They speak of abortion as being the "deliberate termination of a human life"—making it sound like a conscious, calculated murder. "Human life" is also much more personal than "foetus" as one can dismiss a foetus as being too small to count as a life where as "human" makes the foetus sound far more developed and easier to compare to oneself. *Pro-life* refers to unborn babies as being "innocent and defenceless" and alludes to the abuse of abortion and euthanasia laws under Adolf Hitler in Nazi Germany. The latter generates sentiments of disgust and repulsion while the first encourages the audience to feel sympathy for the unborn child and, in turn, campaign against the violent act of abortion. Conversely, anti-abortionists often use the arts to achieve their aims: pictures of aborted babies can lead to strong condemnation of the practice.

Care Not Killing campaigns against euthanasia and speaks about the need to prevent "infanticide" and the "murder of the old". As with abortion, the language used is powerful and emotionally-stimulating. Perhaps the ultimate test of my belief that language plays such an important role when making ethical decisions is the following

---

B The student chooses an authentic and effective example to support the KI that language plays an integral role in ethics. The student identifies lobby group campaigns as demonstrating the emotive power of language. He analyses the terms carefully and also the communication techniques used by the lobby group.

Provide authentic examples that you are able to analyse in detail, revealing how it throws light on the KI.

C Extending the example to show that language can work to communicate and enhance opposing viewpoints increases the analytic nature of the essay. The effectiveness of this example is boosted by the detailed examination of terms and phrases as well as a passing reference to another AOK (history).

↑ Ⓐ Ⓑ

Although hypothetical examples are not generally recommended, this one is effective (B) because it allows exploration of the question of whether language or emotion is ultimately more effective in a highly delicate ethical situation (A).

Avoid using hypothetical examples, unless doing so allows you to explore the finer details of a KI.

↑ Ⓐ

The introduction to a section on a second AOK uses comparison between AOKs to consider the central KI raised by the title. This is followed by consideration of the role of another WOK, reason in the natural sciences; this is compared with the role of language.

Develop breadth of understanding in your discussion of KIs by making comparisons between WOKs and AOKs.

↑ Ⓑ

A very solid and well-explained academic example—binomial nomenclature—is provided to show the fundamental role language has in aspects of the natural sciences. The strength of this example is that knowledge implications are considered, such as the effects of the generalization of knowledge regarding animal species.

hypothetical situation. If I was a doctor, I might have to make a choice between either not resuscitating a dying man—in accordance with his verbal instructions -, or attempting to save his life. Lawfully, the correct decision would be to use the knowledge issue of language and follow his verbal request. Resuscitating him, despite being the action emotion would tell me was correct, would in fact be illegal. Therefore, I believe that in the area of knowledge of ethics, language plays a very important role: both in shaping an opinion and in helping a knower make a lawfully correct decision in an ethical dilemma.

The second area of knowledge I will examine is the natural sciences which, I believe, use language as a way of knowing to a smaller degree than ethics. Natural sciences are the study of the phenomena of the physical universe and use the scientific method as a way of finding explanations and producing theories. The main way of knowing associated with this area of knowledge is, in my opinion, reasoning. This is because the aim of scientific method is to produce a theory, something which can only be deduced from experimentation. Scientists will use reasoning in order to formulate a theory based on an initial hypothesis and subsequent experiments. Language is mostly used once a theory has been established. Binomial nomenclature is used universally to classify animals by naming them in Latin according to their species and genus. Humans are *Homo sapiens*, literally translated as 'the wise man'. *Homo*, the genus, includes humans and their extinct relatives—it is estimated that the Neanderthals died out 30,000 years ago. This process of binomial nomenclature serves several important functions in order that the natural sciences may be taught and the area of knowledge itself may be updated. As the world is full of different languages, an international understanding of an animal or species could potentially be prevented by the knowledge failing to cross international frontiers/By using a common language to name and classify organisms, scientists from all over the world are able to help one another find common patterns between different species, trace their ancestral roots, and develop a greater understanding of the world around them. Charting the evolution of organisms on the planet today will help scientists predict the future of evolutionary activity. Therefore, along with reason, language plays an important role in the natural sciences although its importance is less than in ethics.

The final area of knowledge I will examine is the arts where I believe language plays a significantly smaller role as a way of knowing in comparison to the other two areas I have discussed. The arts cover an incredibly broad spectrum ranging from music to paintings which, for the purpose of my argument, I shall concentrate on. Music, in

G D

This discussion includes several claims and counterclaims, developing an argument (C).

Clarity is enhanced by signalling counterclaims with "however", and implications with "therefore" (D).

Arguments are strengthened by considering claims and counterclaims in relation to an example.

B C

Although this example is good (B), it is not sufficiently analysed (C). The use of the word "story" in the example indicates that it could be counter-argued that the viewer is reading the artwork like a text.

Always look for the possibility of a counterclaim to any claim or example given regarding KIs!

A

The conclusion refers back to the KI expressed in the title. The main arguments and conclusions are summarized, accompanied by evaluation of the central argument and a personal critique.

Apart from being a synopsis of the central arguments, a conclusion also provides an opportunity for you to briefly reflect and evaluate the manner in which you have approached the KIs.

the classical sense, uses very few words and so, in order that it is appreciated and one can use it as an area of knowledge, I believe it uses emotion as particularly forms of music can stimulate emotions. For example, John Williams' musical score for Steven Spielberg's *Schindler's Lists* is commonly accepted to be one of the most heart-wrenching and haunting soundtracks ever to be composed. Given the subject-matter of the film, this seems most appropriate and perhaps the soundtrack is only able to generate such emotion as a result of a listener's perception of the film, which may have been aided by the language. However, I heard the music before seeing the film and yet was still tearful. Evidently, the melody is able to generate emotion without the need of additional ways of knowing. Language is hardly used in classical music as, besides from directions on the manual script such as forte or piano, no words are used. However, here I recognise my own prejudices: my tastes lean towards classical music as opposed to a genre such as rap. In rap music, counter to my previous conclusion, the lyrics employed are deliberately chosen in order to help carry the grievances or opinions of the artist to the listener and so serve the point of the song. Therefore, depending on the area of music in question, language can play a small or a great role of importance.

In another aspect of the arts—drawings and paintings -, perception must be used as this art form requires insight and observation in order to understand the artist's aims and objectives in creating the piece. For example, the Bayeux Tapestry tells the epic tale of the Norman invasion of England in 1066 whilst using very few words. It requires perception to understand the story and learn from it. Therefore, there are large areas of the arts which scarcely use language as a way of knowing as they utilise perception and emotion to a greater degree. However, there are other art forms such as hieroglyphics and the music used by African tribes to communicate which could be argued to be a form of interaction and thus a form of language.

I have examined three areas of knowledge—ethics, natural sciences and the arts—in order to decide whether language plays a role of equal importance between the various areas of knowledge. Using examples from history and my own personal experience, I have argued that language does in fact play roles of different importance in the various areas. As my examples demonstrate, I believe language plays a far greater role in ethics than in the arts or natural sciences. However, I have highlighted the broadness of the arts which will lead rise to disagreement with my conclusion as I have reached it from examining limited, biased examples.

Word Count: 1595

Bibliography

Care not Killing Website: http://www.carenotkilling.org.uk/ 14th June 2007

Klan Parenthood Website: http://www.l00abortionpictures.com/ Aborted_Baby_Pictures_Abortion_Photos/ 14th June 2007

National Abortion Federation Website: http://www.prochoice.org/ 14th June 2007

Pro-Life Alliance Website: http://www.prolife.org.uk/ 14th June 2007

Wikipedia, Neanderthals: http://en.wikipedia.org/wiki/Neanderthal/ 14th June 2007

Examiner report

Criterion A: (9) The essay genuinely explores in a sophisticated manner KIs that are pertinent to the title. The student attempts quite successfully to show that the central KI of the role played by language in the AOKs pragmatically affects the conventions or methodology followed. They also show that it reveals prevailing attitudes and approaches in ethics ("care not killing", euthanasia) and in the natural sciences (binomial nomenclature).

Criterion B: (9) All the examples show an individual approach and the vividness and energy with which they are analysed demonstrates their connection to the student's own experience as a learner. Different perspectives (euthanasia in ethics, film music for Schindler's List) are discussed in depth in order to explore the role of language.

Criterion C: (9) The student develops a critical and insightful inquiry throughout the essay, based upon well-supported claims and examples, with counterclaims balanced by counter-examples (abortion versus pro-choice). Arguments are clear, with main points well justified, while the detail of the analysis allows for the identification of implications and underlying assumptions (particularly in ethics and the natural sciences).

Criterion D: (10) The essay is extremely well structured from the outset, with an overview in the introduction allowing for a clear, overall organization. Concepts are clearly developed and explained, with factual information and well-clarified reasoning to justify argumentation. The referencing permits tracing and acknowledgement of all the sources used.

Overall ...

An excellent essay, in which the student has balanced good organization of ideas with a strong quality of inquiry. How do you think that the examples and viewpoints provided in the essay are relevant to society today? In what manner do the issues and perspectives raised by the essay's discussion address the central KI suggested by the title? Why do you think that it's important to achieve the balance between the ethical, natural sciences and arts AOKs that this essay achieves?

This extract was taken from an essay that achieved 31/40, a grade A (A = 8, B = 8, C = 7, D = 8)

The way in which history is taught is by explaining different interpretations of it, and these exact interpretations are put into words. Therefore it is understandable that language is a crucial element in history as an area of knowledge, since it is essential in order to communicate it. I study history in an international school in the USA, and in my daily school-life I learn how different history can be from what I was taught back home in Israel. I learn how subjective it was and how different wording of the history changes one's perspective. It all depends on what words are chosen to describe and give the facts for the same history. To observe the importance of language in history, take note of the British power in the Middle East since WWI. By using language as their way to manipulate, the British promised the same land to the Jewish and to the Palestinian people. On November 2nd, 1917 in the Balfour Declaration, Arthur James Balfour said "His Majesty's Government view with favour the establishment in Palestine of a national home for the Jewish people, and will use their best endeavours to facilitate the achievement of this object… " About twenty years later on May 17th 1939, the British empire, this time by Malcolm MacDonald published the White Paper of 1939:

His Majesty's Government believe that the framers of the Mandate in which the Balfour Declaration was embodied could not have intended that Palestine should be converted into a Jewish State against the will of the Arab population of the country. […] His Majesty's Government therefore now declare unequivocally that it is not part of their policy that Palestine should become a Jewish State.[1]

From a national home for the Jewish people, Palestine became a Jewish state against the Arabs. This contradiction was so obvious that both the Jewish side and the Palestinian one rejected it. Some supporters of the National Government were opposed to the policy on the grounds that it appeared in their view to contradict the Balfour Declaration. This example is only one of many that show how significant the choice of words is when communicating, depending on what the message one wants to bring across is; whether between nations, groups or individuals.

[1] http://en.wikipedia.org/wiki/White_Paper_of_1939, lasted accessed on 6 December 2007, page was last modified 22:08, 4 December 2007

B

This extract demonstrates a personal approach, introduced by the student's disclosure that they have studied history in two separate countries. The extract shows independent thinking and analysis regarding the role of language in history, such as the interpretation of issues and events. The authentic historical example is particularly relevant to the student's own perspective.

Wherever possible, use examples based upon authentic sources. Examples from your own experience or learning can often be particularly successful.

D

The extract is relevant and well organized. The central KI is clarified and linked clearly to a History AOK context. The factual information used is correct, well researched and properly referenced.

Check the facts and details of any example used. Keep a record of sources accessed so that they can be cited in the references.

In areas of knowledge such as the arts and the sciences, do we learn more from work that follows or that breaks with accepted conventions?

[Title 6, from November 2007/May 2008]

Essay type:

A type 2 title that focuses on two areas of knowledge (arts, science) and requires comparison or contrast between AOKs or across WOKs, looking at a TOK-related term (accepted convention).

Key words and phrases:

- Such as, arts, sciences, do we learn more, follows, breaks, accepted conventions

Contestable concepts:

- Arts, sciences, accepted conventions

  Although you have considered the arts and science in your TOK course, you may well not have talked about "accepted conventions". Developing a clear understanding of the meaning, in the context of the title, of phrases you have not considered in your TOK course is vital to a good answer.

What do you understand by "the arts"? Will you (for example) include literature? How do the arts create new knowledge?

What do you understand by "the sciences"? Will you consider both natural and human sciences? How do the sciences create new knowledge?

Are there situations where the boundaries between art and science are blurred?

What do you understand by "accepted conventions"? Warning: dictionary definitions may be very unhelpful here. Your account of accepted conventions must make sense in the context of the question: that is, they must be the sort of thing that can be followed or broken, and both must be capable of leading to new knowledge.

Are accepted conventions different in the arts from in the sciences?

Ambiguous terms

- We, follows, breaks

Does "we" refer to all of humanity, or to some smaller group of which you are a member?

What do you think is meant by work that follows (or breaks) accepted conventions? Is it about what is done, the way of doing it, the conclusions that emerge, or something else (or a mixture of all these)?

In what manner could we learn from these kinds of work?

Action terms

- do we learn more, such as

  You are being asked to decide, on the basis of your discussion, which approach gains us greater knowledge in the AOKs you considered—though you might conclude that both are essential. The phrase "such as" indicates that you may consider only these two AOKs, these two plus one or two others, or some different set of AOKs.

Assumptions in the title

That in both the arts and the sciences it is easy to distinguish work that follows, from work that breaks with, accepted conventions.

That the answer whether we learn more from work that follows or that breaks with accepted conventions is the same for both the arts and the sciences.

Will you contest these assumptions?

Rephrase the title to check your understanding

You can check your understanding of the title by rewriting it in a manner similar to the one below.

- When working at the cutting edge of knowledge, is it more fruitful to take the approach that others have taken before, or to try a new, different approach?

This is just one way the question could be rewritten. It sees the conventions as approaches taken by experts, and "we" as all humanity. Your unpacking of the terms may be different from this.

Identify the knowledge issues

- How easy is it to identify whether a piece of work follows or breaks with conventions?

- Do both approaches to learning have their own essential strengths?

- Can it be the case that conventional or classical ways of doing things can seem so expert as to be inaccessible except to the very able or talented learners? Is it easier to learn from work that does not require conventional approaches and methods?

- Is it useful to think of work that breaks accepted convention to be a "paradigm shift" such as a new art movement or a scientific revolution?

Brainstorming

Consider WOKs and AOKs

The title mentions two AOKs, the arts and the sciences. Although this does not make it compulsory, it is a good idea, at least initially, to identify and consider examples from the contexts of these two AOKs.

Do the nature and implications of work that follows accepted conventions and work that breaks them differ between the arts and the sciences? Can you evaluate and compare the results and effects of work that follows conventions in the arts and the sciences contrasted with work that breaks with it?

What part do WOKs play in the manner in that accepted conventions in the sciences or the arts support, justify and establish knowledge?

Will you deal with arts and sciences in general, or will you look at particular arts and sciences?

Will you consider another AOK? Would you rather talk only about some other AOKs? What about in other AOKs such as history, ethics or mathematics? Will you explore any of them?

Make claims and develop perspectives using authentic examples to illustrate and support your discussion

What advantages, and disadvantages, can you see in doing work that follows conventions?

What advantages, and disadvantages, can you see in doing work that breaks conventions?

What examples can you provide of situations in which a learning process can be related to conventional work or work that breaks conventions? Think of the advances and discoveries you have studied in your IB subjects, or come across on TV, in your reading, at exhibitions, in the cinema, on the internet etc.

Do you have any personal experiences of your own work that follows or breaks with conventions?

Analyse and argue

Provide effective counterclaims, counter-arguments and counter-examples to support them.

Is "unlearning" and a revolutionary rejection of previous learning a necessary stage in the learning process in the long term? You could consider the relevance of Kuhn's theory of scientific revolution whereby older scientific conventions and theories are rejected and replaced by new ones.

Are all revolutionary approaches fruitful?

Evaluate and conclude

Do your conclusions vary according to whether you are considering the arts or science?

What about other AOKs—will your conclusion apply to them?

Do your conclusions vary according to the criteria used for learning or the "type" or "style" of learning?

Is the opposition created by contrasting following and breaking conventions misleading? Are they dependent upon one another in learning and knowledge processes?

This essay achieved 13/40, a grade D

D The student has paraphrased the title, and hence fails to address what is meant by "accepted conventions", or which approach is better for learning.

Avoid changing or shortening the prescribed title. Doing so risks producing an essay that fails to respond to all aspects of the title.

D In the second paragraph, the student finally refers to a KI raised by the title; however, without much clarification. The discussion is difficult to follow. The generalization regarding the fate of those breaking conventions is factually incorrect.

Early in the essay, clarify the relevant KIs. Check that your writing will be understood. Short, sharp sentences are good. Check your facts. Avoid wild generalizations.

B Although this example is appropriate, the student's treatment is very generalized. The student does not relate the example to the broader argument.

Breaking Convention into the World Unknown

Stem cell research, cloning, abstract pieces of work that extend beyond the limits that human society had once thought possible. As the things that were once thought only possible in Science Fiction come off the pages created by artists and into reality created by scientists, humanity is just beginning to realize just how far we can extend out boundaries. Our capability to cure humanities insatiable curiosity scares a lot of people, they fear that the new technology and the advancing front of scientific discovery will destroy older methods that set the standard for many different discoveries.

Some of the worlds greatest discoveries and monuments have come from people wishing to break free from the accepted terms of the world around them and create something new and different. However, most of these people who wished to break free from conventions set up by the societies of the time, conventions who's fundamental tenet is that all knowledge rests on either authority or reason and whatever is deduced from reason depends ultimately upon a premise derived from authority, were met with injustice and death.

Some of the theories made in the past are still being debated today, like Charles Darwin's theory of Evolution. A theory presented in the eighteen hundreds, after Charles Darwin studied animals on the Galapagos Islands, stating that the organisms we see around us today, including humans, evolved from less complex organisms as the environment pushed for certain characteristics. This idea however was shunned by the current trend of the time, the trend of creationism, that God created all as a part of one great design. The religious community met Darwins' theory with scepticism and criticism on all fronts; fervent in their efforts to prevent anything that would state that their theory of God creating all could be false. Today the battle between creationism and Darwinism is still going on, the premises over which the battle is being fought might have changed but the overall fight is still the same.

> The discussion here is too general and lacks specific information to justify and clarify the claims made. The student makes some analogies such as the "system crashing"; these are unsupported by any facts or context. This makes it very difficult to understand them or to apply them to the KIs addressed in the essay's introduction.

As humans we wish to hold onto some kind of belief that determines what we do and how we act in the world around us. When confronted with new and different we will fight against it or our natural curiosity will kick in and we will want to figure out what the new thing is. The mixture of possible reactions that a person can have to any new idea is what holds back the majority of our discoveries and causes the better proportion of many scientific arguments. As complex as the human brain may be there are a few things that it cannot compensate for and when shocked with something abnormally new and different the brain doesn't know how to cope. It is for this reason that many new discoveries are slowly eased into the general public so that the system around which human society revolves won't crash from an over stimulus.

The methods used to introduce new ideas are more often than not conventional methods, but that's because they have been proven to work. Conventional has been tested against unconventional time and time again to see which ones work better and which ones are going to be more readily accepted by the people. It is because conventional methods clash with unconventional methods that the world today is advancing as quickly as it is. Conventional methods like the scientific method help keep people within a certain comfort zone that allows them to piece through most problems and come up with a reasonable conclusion, like getting too close to a fire without cause pain while staying at a certain distance from a flame can be beneficial. Conventional science and ideas help us cope with the world that we already know because those methods and ideas have been proven to get valid outcomes that benefit the individual. When something contradicts the conventional people are then forced to start thinking.

> This is a typical case of an unsupported claim in the essay. The claim itself is an interesting one, but without an example to justify and clarify it, the reader has no context in which to consider details, characteristics and/or implications of the claim.

> This is the only example used in the essay that is developed to anything near to a satisfactory extent; however, it is unclear in places. Mentioning that both sides have strong points is no substitute for exploring those points. Would the overall example be more effective if authentic stem cell research news stories or similar had been included?

Stem cell research is probably one of the best examples of conventional methods being tested against unconventional methods and something much more profitable is created from the chaos. As an issue steeped in moral debate, stem cell research has been one of the most controversial projects ever made. On the more conventional side, people are saying that stem cell research is killing human embryos before they can even become fully aware of themselves. On the other, slightly less conventional side, people are saying that stem cell research is just a small step necessary to the further research and development of cures for diseases like cancer and sickle cell anemia and for disabilities like paralysis and Parkinson's disease. Both sides have very strong points to be made, and the debates have reached a point that most governments won't fund anyone who wishes to research stem cells. This isn't entirely a bad thing.

Because researchers can't get the funding that they need to further their studies on stem cells, or young human embryos, they have had to come up with a different way to get to the place that they need to be to completely their research, without "killing" an embryo. What do we get? Dedifferentiation, a normal cell process that our cells go through during their normal life cycle, merely reversed. Scientists are now able to get the king of cells that they need to research without causing problems with the moral of killing an embryo

Whether it is conventional methods that help to keep everyone following a similar path or an unconventional method that challenges what we already think we know, advancing the world that we know around us is simply a matter of what we're willing to listen to.

The Fixation of Belief, Writing of Charles S. Peirce, 1872- 1878

The Origin of the Species, Charles Darwin, 1859

*Notes from the Genetics Conference held at Lubbock High School, in Lubbock Texas

Word Count: 937

A The conclusion provides neither a synopsis nor an evaluation of the claims and arguments. Nor does it refer to the terms in the title.

Your conclusion should wrap up your argument and refer back to the KI in the title.

D The references are not presented in a standard fashion, and do not allow tracing of the sources.

Use a standard citation system for references.

D The essay does not reach 1,200 words and hence cannot gain more than 4 marks under criterion D.

Ensure your word count lies between 1,200 and 1,600 words.

Examiner report

Criterion A: (3) The student expresses some quite outspoken opinions; however, these views are so unsupported and unqualified that they can barely be considered as claims that are relevant to KIs deriving from the title. The student sometimes seems to approach KIs through examples, but these are not sufficiently well developed to allow adequate treatment of KIs.

Criterion B: (3): Although some examples used (Darwin—evolution) are appropriate for the exploration of KIs under discussion, the student's treatment of the example is too vague and broad. Generally, examples are not sufficiently connected to context. Even when examples are developed to a more satisfactory extent, they are not explored or explained in sufficient detail.

Criterion C: (3) The discussion that the student develops in this essay is too general and lacks specific information to justify claims made. Even the seemingly more relevant and interesting claims are not sufficiently justified by clarification and supportive examples; neither does the student provide the counterclaims and counter-examples necessary to ensure a good quality of analysis.

Criterion D: (4) The essay has a limited overall organization and it is often difficult to appreciate the student's intention in the case of examples, argumentation and discussion of KIs that are attempted. The essay is also poorly structured since the student does not provide an adequate introduction or conclusion. The student does not comply with the word count since the essay has a word count of only 937 words, hence not able to gain more than 4 marks under criterion D.

Overall …

The essay has lost marks on account of the poor development of ideas and discussion. How could the student have more adequately addressed KIs implied by the title? Could key terminology such as "learn" and "conventions" have been explored? Could the student have provided examples that helped show self-awareness as a knower? What examples from the arts and the sciences would you choose in order to help to provide a successful critical inquiry into KIs raised by the title?

This essay achieved 18/40, a grade C

A

The introduction repeats the original title, but does not identify the central KIs or indicate how the student understands the task.

Present your interpretation of the title in your own words, and support it. Briefly but clearly indicate the central KIs that the essay is going to address.

D

The student defines the key term "learn" by giving four dictionary definitions, without discussing them or indicating which will be used in the essay.

Avoid repeating dictionary definitions. Rather, clarify and explore the concepts to which the terms refer. It is good discuss their meaning through a context or example relevant to the title.

In this essay, I will answer the question whether or not we learn more from works that follow or that breaks with the accepted conventions in the areas of knowledge such as the arts and the sciences. In order to comprehensively answer this question, it is of outmost importance to first define the key word "learn". Then, it is also vital to separately examine both areas of knowledge as they are both unique to each other. I will also be sharing my personal experiences that are relevant to this question.

Definition of the word "learn":

- "The act, process, or experience of gaining knowledge or skill."[1]
- "Knowledge or skill acquired by instruction or study."[2]
- "to acquire knowledge of or skill in by study, instruction, or experience"[3]
- "to become informed"[4]

Now with these definitions in mind, we can now continue in the discussion of the main question: **"In areas of knowledge such as the arts and the sciences, do we learn more from, work that follows or that breaks with accepted conventions?"**

D The student makes an attempt to explain "accepted conventions" but the discussion lacks clarity because the phrase is not made the centre of the discussion.

Early in an essay, key concepts raised by the title need to be explicitly clarified and explored.

A The student identifies a relevant KI here, helpfully introducing a historical perspective on science.

Use opportunities that present themselves to explore a KI through different knowledge perspectives.

B This good example, which gives a historical perspective on scientific change, is treated in too simplistic a manner. The observation about chemistry is not clarified or explained at all.

Use examples as opportunities to develop consideration of knowledge perspectives into a fuller exploration of KIs.

C These interesting counterclaims need further development in order to analyse relevant KIs.

Develop ideas and examples with depth and breadth and link them explicitly to the KI.

It is my personal opinion that if we humans were to learn and discover or even experience new things, it is necessary to go over and beyond the accepted norms that we ourselves have established. Although this method entails a process of trial and error, I believe it is worth investigating the probabilities that might or might not be for our own benefit. This is because regardless of the outcome, we would either way learn more.

The study of science demands the process of investigation. This is how we discover the complex workings of the things that surround us. It is through this method that we can manage to explain and understand the phenomenons that occur in our daily lives. There are but only two options that we have in order for us to progress in our pursuit in the study of science. One of these options is to build on the knowledge that we already have acquired. The alternative option is for us to debunk the knowledge that we have already held on to and try to find a more appropriate or even a "new" explanation.

All throughout the history, in the field of science, and even at present, there have been instances where accepted theories that have been established for years and are believed to be truths, are disproved. Although many of those who had disproved the accepted norms rarely met a positive feedback from society. Take for example Nicolas Copernicus. During his era, the accepted fact was that the earth was the stationary and that the sun would revolve around it, this was called the geocentric theory.[5] However, Copernicus disproved this and concluded that it was the other way around. His theory, the heliocentric theory[6], profoundly revolutionized how people view the universe. In the early years if chemistry, several molecular models have been developed in an attempt to explain the nature of the "thing" that our world consists of.[7]

However, it could also possibly be argued that there exist new theories in science that are developed because of further studying the established conventions without debunking its integrity. Galileo Galilee, the father of modem observational astronomy[8], for instance studied the heliocentric theory of our universe that was developed by Nicolas Copernicus and through this he was able to learn more regarding the structure of our universe. Another good example of this is the equation that made Albert Einstein, $E = mc^2$. Einstein was able to develop this equation with the use of the knowledge that have already been established earlier.

In regards to the other area of knowledge in question, art, where creativity is of outmost importance, I believe that it is almost impossible for it to progress and for us to experience or discover new things if

B This is an original example that shows the student taking an individual approach. He considers the contrast between two "schools of art" as a good vehicle through which to explore the KIs raised by the title in an authentic context.

C D This paragraph describes the changes but does little to explore them in relation to the KI from the title. It is also not the case that impressionism was replaced by realism. It's quite unclear what the student means by this erratic information.

In order to consider relevant KIs adequately, fully interrogate viewpoints and examples. Factual claims should present information that is correct and supported by reference to a source.

B This example (revisited further down) clearly connects the concepts and the KIs in the title to the student's own experience as a learner, with careful attention to detail, and genuine and effective exploration of the central KIs.

Include well-analysed examples that focus on your own experience as a learner.

the established conventions are not broken. Since creativity entails originality and new ways to express one's self. Although compared to science, the way we learn through art has a more subtle nature. Take for example paintings and sculptures. If one would, let us say, compare the pieces of work in Europe before and after the Firsts World war, one would not fail to notice a radical difference in both eras. Before and after the First World War, it was impressionism that flourished and dominated the art scene. Picturesque scenes would be what one would commonly encounter in this era. However, in the years following the war, impressionism was abandoned, in other words debunking.. Impressionism as a form of art was considered to be hypocrisy. This was then replaced with another form of art which we now know today as realism. Now all those picturesque scenes have disappeared and were then replaced with paintings and sculptures that depicts a theme; the world is not perfect.

Just like in the field of science, it still could be argued that it is possible to learn new things through building on the accepted conventions. Take dancing for instance. It is not too difficult to see how dancing has evolved all throughout the years. From ancient tribal dances to ballet and to the modern dances that we have today, it is very evident that all of them have similar movements to a certain degree. The difference is that these movements are executed in several manners and also with a different tempo.

Personal experience

I used to be a very competitive chess player during my teen years; I competed almost every weekend and won numerous awards. In chess, there are two types of players. One can choose to be an AGGRESSIVE or a POSITIONAL player. Both types have very different approach to the game. The aggressive player would prefer to have an "open" position for easy manoeuvrability of the pieces while the positional player would prefer a "close" or cramped position. I started off as an aggressive player in the beginning. However, as the years went by, I changed my playing style from aggressive to positional. It was very hard at first since the approach in playing the game as a positional player is very different. However, with more practice I was able grasp the ideas behind this type of approach and was able to adapt them in my games. From then on I noticed that my playing skills had improve tremendously in such a short span of time. I do not believe that it was because I was gifted but because by the time I was able to understand the methods that both type of playing strategy employed, my understanding of the dynamics of the game broadened. As a result, I grew as a player. I was able to achieve this by breaking the conventions that I exercised and by exploring the ideas behind positional play. If I stayed as a an aggressive player throughout the years, I highly doubt the possibility of me growing as a strong player.

A very good example on learning through following accepted conventions was when I started going to school in first grade. I learned back then the four basic mathematical operations. These are addition, subtraction, multiplication and division. As I progressed on my academic life, mathematics became more and more challenging. Things started to get more complicated after algebra, geometry, trigonometry, logarithms, calculus, probabilities and statistics were introduced. However, learning all these topics would have been impossible if I had not learned the four basic mathematical operations since the basic priciples of these different topics require prior knowledge regarding the our basic operations.

To generalize, looking back on the example regarding chess, I was able to improve my playing skills by going against the conventions that I first accepted. And because I went against it, I was able to see the "other side" of the game. It is suffice to say that I was able to learn more because by the time I knew both playing styles, my understanding of the game was extended. Now regarding the example that deals with mathematics, I was able to expand my knowledge in this field by building through established conventions. There exist no other way of learning mathematics if one cannot learn and implement the basic principles.

Now back to the question. Yes it is true that we can learn regardless if we build on the conventions that we have acquired or debunk it and create something new. But the question specifies whether we learn more or less on both methods. I stand behind what was stated earlier that we can learn more if we break the current convention in both the sciences and arts. Put it simply like this (the road will be a metaphor for knowledge); if we build on our existing conventions, it is like building a straight road. We do nothing else but keep building that same road continuously from where it had previously stopped. This of course entails progress in learning if we based it on the definition of the word "learn" since new portion of the road is continually built.. However, if we choose create new roads from the straight road that we have built, then we will find that we have built a road that branches out in many different ways, thus learning more compared to the one dimensional road which is the straight one.

C

The counter-argument is instanced well through this example. However, the argument here could be more explicitly linked to the general KI.

Ensure that counter-arguments are effective by supporting them with carefully chosen examples, then stating the implications.

D

The conclusion revisits the main KIs raised by the title and, for the first time, addresses the issue concerning which methods lead to learning more effectively.

The conclusion of a TOK essay can be more than simply a synopsis of the main claims and perspectives. It can contribute to the evaluation of central KIs. Nevertheless, it should not be the first place new material is introduced.

Bibliography Websites:

1 http://education.yahoo.com/reference/dictionary/entry/learning, jan 11 2008, 16:04

2 http://www.m-w.comldictionaryllearning.jan 11 2008, 16:10

3 http://dictionary.reference.com/browse/learn. jan 11 2008, 16: 113

4 ibid

5 http://www.blupete.com/Literature/Biographies/Science/Copernicus.htm. November 15 2007, 15:29

6 http://www.blupete.com/Literature/Biographies/Science/Copernicus.htm. November 15 2007, 15:29

7 http://www.iadeaf.k12.ia.us/The%20Atomic%20Model.htm. November 15 2007,16:00

8 http://www.Iucidcafe.com/library/96feb/galileo.html. November 16, 12:00

Examiner report

Criterion A: (4) The essay demonstrates more understanding of relevant KIs as it progresses. Following a rather simplistic and derived beginning, the student moves towards developing their own perspectives and more original examples. This allows for a more insightful examination of related KIs such as whether it is necessary to break conventions in order to achieve creativity and originality in the arts. The chess game example successfully allows for exploration of the KI of which approach regarding conventions is most relevant to "learning".

Criterion B: (5) Although the knower's perspective is not very evident at the start of the essay, the student engages in an increasingly personal manner as the essay progresses. The section on arts AOK takes an interesting historical perspective that allows examination of the central KI. The student explores his personal experience of learning in great detail through the chess example, which is strong in terms of independent thinking. Examples chosen are generally good; however, in general the student does not analyse them in sufficient detail.

Criterion C: (4) The best quality of analysis in the essay is related to the exploration of examples and personal perspectives. It is only once the student begins to develop these that he is able to explore rather than just describe the KIs. Unfortunately the student does not do this enough, neither does he provide sufficient counterclaims.

Criterion D: (5) Although the structure of the essay is satisfactory, there are parts, in particular the early section of the essay, where the use of language sometime hampers the reader's understanding. In the later part of the essay, the development of examples provides material to support perspectives and arguments regarding the KIs. Although most sources of information and ideas are acknowledged and most referencing allows tracing of the sources used, there are some factual inaccuracies such as the comment about impressionism.

Overall ...

This essay only just reaches satisfactory and a C grade. It demonstrates how important it is in a TOK essay for the student not just to include examples, but to include ones which develop perspectives that vividly and genuinely show the student's self-awareness as a knower. How effectively do you think the student uses examples and viewpoints to shape the essay in a way that shows thoughtful, personal engagement with the KIs? How would you have developed more detailed analysis and provided more counter-examples and counterclaims? How would you suggest this essay be developed beyond a "satisfactory" quality to a "good" one?

This essay achieved 39/40, a grade A

A

The student identifies and explores the key phrase "accepted conventions" and immediately includes other terms from the title. The central KI is further clarified by involving other contestable knowledge concepts not mentioned in the title, such as truth. The student also makes links to methodologies in the relevant AOKs and to the learning process referred to in the title.

In the introduction of your TOK essay, clarify the KIs right from the outset! Identify and address key terms in order to reveal and clarify relevant KIs and related knowledge controversies.

B

By examining a shift in music conventions, the example highlights the context of an AOK to explore the KI concerning how humans learn best. The student clearly connects his own personal learning experience to the KI. The student also fully examines the effects of the shift in musical convention on musicians worldwide. The student shows an ability to get inside and appreciate other knowers' perspectives.

When using an extended example, consider carefully and in detail the situations it provides. This maximizes the example's potential to explore perspectives on KIs.

We, as human beings, take the work done in the past as the truth and are unwilling to question it since we see the work in the world around us and we understand the world through these accepted conventions. When work is done differently, we see it as 'breaking from convention' and therefore should not be trusted because we see change as not only putting a change on the one convention, but on all the conventions we hold close and causes us to question all the conventions we have in place. The implication of conventions is that people begin to see the convention as the only truth. In many cases, like in the arts, the truth is all through an individual's personal interpretation and there is therefore no simple 'right' answer. With sciences, the break from convention usually is more extreme—usually something is proven wrong so we learn that our way of thinking must shift. Therefore, we need to start to see what factors are being used to influence the way people create the work we learn from. The knowledge issue is what are the factors that influence the need for security in how we learn from work that follows or breaks with accepted conventions?

Music, like all art, has changed throughout time as techniques and focuses change. In 6th grade I learned about the progression of musical instruments. When the instruments improve, like the shift from harpsichord to the modem piano was able to become more dynamic, the type of music will also create a new shift from what was expected. There is therefore a way of knowing, reasoning, caused this shift from the Baroque period to the Classical period, since the instruments now have the ability to use dynamics more than were able to use them in the past. This work did not have a sudden transition and was accepted by society. The transition happened by more modem instruments playing in the pieces, like pianos replacing harpsichords in the orchestra, and slowly adding more and more dynamics to the pieces. This shows how that the break of convention can be accepted and can allow for new artistic events to take their course further down the road.

While learning music theory in 10th grade I learned about the shift between the Baroque and the Classical period, once again. This time, I learned about how the classical period of music was where more melodies are used but also how a piece is more likely to stick to one emotion, rather than the baroque period where there were a variety of emotions represented in one piece. In the Classical period, there is one major climax in a piece and the piece ends quietly, which is very unlike the music created in the Baroque period. This therefore means that emotion was used in deciding how to play these new pieces and caused composers like Christopher Willibald Gluck[1], who started the use of powerful dramatic shifts, to break from the conventions that were used for almost 150 years. This shift allows musicians worldwide to have the opportunity to place new music with more dynamic variation within their new pieces. The progressions continue to take place within the musical community and though they are not accepted always at the start of the period, they can be the beginning of something that lasts for centuries. The people that do not accept the new and different pieces are usually conservatives that believe that music is fine the way it is. They don't try to see that there may be good pieces from different periods of music and from using different methods of playing. Even though the new period has created a new way of representing the truth, some people do not feel comfortable being a part of a new period.

There are some composers though who have seen the importance of keeping to the conventions set before them. Bach, a highly regarded composer, realized the importance of the features of old techniques, from the Baroque period, and has found a way to incorporate them into his pieces in the Classical period. This has caused a stir for many musicians because the shift for many others was to reject the techniques from the past whereas he used them to create the most out of his pieces. The gain for knowledge in this case is how a mix can be created between the work that fits old conventions and also utilizes the new conventions. The ability to change our convention has not prevented people from playing pieces from the Baroque period and has just allowed a new era to start.

Paradigms are a set of assumptions that create a way of viewing reality. These paradigms can change and cause a shift in the way we view life in general, making us lose the security we have of understanding some of the world around us. Paradigms include the earth being shaped in the shape of a sphere and the earth revolving around the sun. My next example is an isolated paradigm that caused a shift in the way people in a village in Togo think. In 1978, my dad worked as a Peace Corps volunteer in northern Togo. He was the only person in the village with a refrigerator where he was able to make ice cubes in the heat of the country. One of the Togolese boys saw the ice and touched it and ran to go show it to his friends. He tried multiple times to run the ice all the way to his friends but could not understand why the ice kept turning into water. The idea of freezing an object to make it into another state of matter had never been recognized within the village. This was a step in their understanding of the wider world. They were then able to learn about the relationship between temperature and the speed at

This counterclaim takes the form of a counter-example, which allows details of the KI to be considered in a real-life setting.

It is often useful to use a counter-example to explore a counterclaim. This can help you consider authentic details that reveal the complexities of a KI.

This illustrates well how the skilful use of an authentic example can satisfy all four assessment criteria. The personal example, with its link to paradigms and its cultural reference, is particularly strong in terms of knower's perspectives (B). Strong links are made to learning (A). It analyses in detail the process whereby an accepted convention is broken to allow the way for a paradigm shift (C). Terms are used clearly and precisely in a well-organized approach (D).

which the molecules within them move. This therefore was a shift in their convention of understanding using deductive reasoning to follow the heat and what product is created. This paradigm shows how new knowledge can be found that does break with accepted conventions by using reasoning, based on experience. After learning how it takes place scientifically people are willing to accept it as their new paradigm. There has not been a loss of security from this new paradigm; they now just have a new factor that hadn't been necessary before and have a way of now explaining the relation between water and ice.

People see science as a backing of their ideas, with constants, variables, a specific methodology, and quantitative (seemingly unbiased) results, most people believe what is said at the conclusion of an experiment. Within the science community there has been a lot of battles over global warming. The work being done by businesses, like Exxon, do not always lead to the same results shown by independent scientists. The ties that the oil businesses have to global warming are not very positive and have been accused for confusing the general public into not following the research being done by other scientists who give evidence for global warming. Gas companies, like Exxon, have 'misrepresented the science of climate change by outright denial of the evidence'[2]. This accusation is because third-parties see the link between the gas companies and global warming—if global warming is an accepted convention gas companies lose their business. This shows how denial is usually directly linked to breaking with old conventions. This shows the flaw of using emotion while creating work scientifically.

People have seen this perspective and because not believing in global warming would allow people to not be affected and not have to change their conventions, people are willing to believe the information given by these gas companies without question.

Al Gore and the other members of the United Nations (UN) Intergovernmental Panel on Climate Change have taken a different approach to the climate change. They have bound themselves emotionally in their work and are in desperate search for solutions to fix, or at least minimize, the problem. These scientists have increased the productivity of solar and hydroelectric energy, a way to minimize the use of fossil fuels. This can be seen as a really positive change that has been caused by the emotional addition to the scientific work. The work is reliable, with more data and arguments in favor of global warming but is a break with accepted conventions, so people are more unwilling to agree with it.

D The brief summary of the traditional scientific approach helps to set the context for the subsequent controversial example.

Careful planning of the ordering of claims, examples and counter-examples improves critical discussion.

B This example counters the view of science as unbiased and unemotional, by exploring new factors such as industry ties and denial.

C The student identifies the implications. This considerably strengthens the argumentation and also the quality of the inquiry in the essay.

B Providing another perspective shows a different attitude to convention within the context of AOKs natural and human science, and WOK emotion.

Use authentic counter-examples to examine alternative perspectives, enabling consideration of the complex interaction of AOKs and WOKs that are often not shown by hypothetical examples.

This short conclusion is a successful synopsis and evaluation of the essay's central claims.

A synopsis and brief evaluation of your claims, tied to the KI raised by the title, can be the core of an effective conclusion.

The referencing of sources used in the essay is partial and probably a reason for a lost mark. Personal examples such as the Togolese ice one need no reference. However, the music examples do.

Reference sources for any claims that are not common knowledge and when using web sources such as websites or weblogs (blogs) include the date accessed.

These examples all show a way that people have reacted to a break in conventions. In most cases, a deciding factor is based on the security one is losing by this new convention. With music, we see that it is easier to shift conventions, since old pieces can still be played. With science, when a convention is changed it usually means that something before was wrong and our way of viewing life has to change. Therefore, we need to be willing to question the works that we learn from and not take everything as the truth, whether or not it falls in or out of accepted conventions.

WORD COUNT: 1,572

Bibliography

Goldberg: http://www.goldbergweb.com/en/history/composers/11010.php (26/01/08)

Guardian: http://www.guardian.co.uk/environment/2006/sep/20/oilandpetrol.business (20/09/06)

Examiner report

Criterion A: (10) The student addresses KIs right from the start of the essay by examining key terms and concepts in the title. The key KI of which approach regarding conventions best achieves learning is treated in depth, especially through the student's exploration of cultural situations (Togo) and subjects (music) he has studied. The student elaborates very effective links between AOKs and WOKs (for example between science, politics and emotion).

Criterion B: (10) The student has approached the essay in a very independent manner and shaped it in a manner that shows significant self-awareness as a knower. The examples chosen through which to develop investigation into the KIs are original and well developed in depth. The connection the student makes between the Togo response to ice and the concept of a paradigm is particularly successful in revealing detailed aspects of the nature of learning, a key KI. The analysis of the climate change example is sophisticated and valuable thanks to its very current significance to contemporary society.

Criterion C: (10) The student uses examples and contexts to explore the central KIs in great detail and depth. Care is taken to support and justify claims with examples and factual information. The student provides effective counterclaims, especially through contrasting perspectives within different AOKs (music, climate change). There is also evaluation provided of the underlying implications and assumptions that emerge with the development of arguments (climate change).

Criterion D: (9) The essay is well structured and the ideas and arguments very well developed. The student uses concepts very clearly, providing helpful examples, explanations and relevant information. Why do you think a mark was taken from this criterion? Do you think it could be on account of inadequate referencing of sources? Of course it can be argued that where examples are very personal, that there will be a lack of sources, however this may not be the case here.

Overall ...

A particularly rewarding essay to read, especially because of the variety and relevance of the situations and contexts that the student explores in order to consider the KI. How does the student relate a keen awareness of cultural, political and environmental situations to the central KIs raised by the title? Do you consider that this essay satisfies the four essay assessment criteria in a balanced manner?

(A) (B)

Personal engagement with the KI is shown through detailed analysis of a particular writer, neatly showing how Kerouac firstly accepted and then broke conventions. These considerations are well tied to the AOK (the arts: literature) and to changing cultural and historical paradigms and conditions.

Solid analysis of an example you know well demonstrates both your personal engagement and your grasp of the KI.

Nonetheless, stylistic literary paradigms have occurred. For instance, romanticism was followed by realism, which represented an existential investigation of reality during a period when industrialization and scientific discoveries permeated Western civilization. Literature thus reflects the combination of a writer's influence by his predecessors and his emotional interpretation of his contemporaries. In post-war America, the author Jack Kerouac published his first novel *The Town and The City* (1950)—a reflection of the contemporary agonies and joys of the American youth. However, it was just that: a reflection, not the innovative work of an "architect of change". Kerouac's style was heavily imitative of Thomas Wolfe [1], and showed little originality. In such a case, literature is shaped by the contemporaries—not the opposite.

On the contrary, Kerouac's second novel *On The Road* (1957) was stylistically revolutionary. It was written with highly unconventional sentence structure and rhythm. Kerouac explained, "I got sick and tired of the conventional English sentence […] so ironbound in its rules, so inadmissible with reference to the actual format of my mind."[2] The essence is that there was a need for a different mode of expression; a need for a new literary paradigm. The nature of paradigm shifts is such that they occur when old conventions do not suffice in an environment that has changed.

Kerouac therefore relinquished his Wolfe imitations. Regina Weinreich, professor in Humanities, has compared Kerouac's language in *On The Road* to the structure of jazz music, entailing an avoidance of language "riddled by false colons" and "needless commas". Kerouac used rhetoric similar to the improvisational composition of jazz music.[3] He called his style 'spontaneous prose', implying that any text produced would correspond directly to the flow of his thoughts and remain unrevised. Literature will hence be affected by the author's subconscious emotions, rather than the reason behind the content.

The *modus operandi* that Kerouac hereby introduced inspired many, but never diminished the importance of traditional literature. Rather: Kerouac personally could not express his creativity through conventional modes, but conventional literature had been shaped by a long process of literary development and hence adapted to

1 Weinstein, Regina, Kerouac's *Spontaneous Poetics—a Study of Fiction*, Thunder's Mouth Press, 1987, p.4
2 Weinstein, Kerouac's Spontaneous Poetics—a study of the fiction, p.2
3 Weinstein, Kerouac's Spontaneous Poetics—a study of the fiction, p.42

mainstream culture as a comprehensible mode of expression. Traditionalists emotionally rejected Kerouac's style, which rejected their inherited culture.[4] He was criticized on the grounds of appeal to tradition. However, in an ever-changing civilization, where societal paradigms shift, the mentality of young generations tend to change and counter-cultures emerge. Kerouac's literature not only reflected this phenomenon, but also amplified it. Arts reflect societal trends, but in cases as revolutionary as that of Kerouac's, it might also be the reason behind such trends. At the very least, it causes re-evaluation of existing conventions. In my own reading of Kerouac, I experienced how the *Verfremdungseffekt* caused by the unconventional structure awakened my consciousness as a reader.

---

4   Clark, Tom, *Jack Kerouac—A Biography*, Plexus Publishing Unlimited, London, 1984, p.108

Kit 4

Our senses tell us that a table, for example, is a solid object; science tells us that the table is mostly empty space. Thus two sources of knowledge generate conflicting results. Can we reconcile such conflicts?

[Title 7, from November 2007/May 2008]

Essay type:

A type 4 title that focuses on an example (the table as solid or empty space) to be explored by reference to AOKs (science, others of your choice) and WOKs (sense perception, others of your choice) and a TOK-related term (reconciling conflicting results).

Key words and phrases:

- senses, solid object, science; empty space; sources of knowledge; reconcile; such; conflicting results

Contestable concepts

- Senses, science, sources of knowledge

How do the senses tell us a table is solid?

How does science tell us it is mostly empty space?

Are the sources of knowledge limited to the AOKs and WOKs?

Ambiguous terms

- Solid object, empty space

How will you understand the claim that a table is *solid* to the senses?

How will you understand the claim that a table is mainly *empty* space to a scientist?

Action terms

- Such, can we reconcile

You are being asked to make a judgment on whether these two knowledge claims—and other such pairs where different sources of knowledge seem to say different things—really are incompatible. Notice that the word "such" does allow you to discuss similar conflicts, and not this specific one.

Assumptions in the title

- That there really is a conflict

Are these statements really in conflict?

Is there ever a genuine conflict when two sources of knowledge seem to make incompatible claims?

Rephrase the title to check your understanding

Having thought about all the above, now is the time for you to make sure you understand the intent of the whole title. Here is an attempt to rephrase it:

- If we say we can't push our hands through a table, but scientists say the table is made of atoms with tiny nuclei and large electron orbits, must one of these statements be false? Would that be the case whenever the ways we seek understanding give us different accounts?

Note that this is just one way the question could be rewritten, and that it relies on an understanding of solidity as being about touch, and of empty space as depending on atomic structure. Your unpacking of these two terms may be different from this.

Identify knowledge issues

Having clarified to your own satisfaction what the title is asking, you should now be able to identify the knowledge issue(s) which you will target in your essay. Based on the above rewriting of the title, we might come up with several:

- Do our senses give us certain knowledge about the way the world is? Why, or why not?

- Does science give us certain knowledge about the way the world is? Why, or why not?

- How can we work out what to believe when different inquiries do not agree?

- How can the interpretation of empirical evidence produced by the senses be compared with the interpretation of theoretical knowledge claims?

- Can the language we use to describe things mislead us?

Brainstorming

Consider WOKs and AOKs

This title specifically mentions one WOK (sense perception) and one AOK (natural science). An obvious starting point is to deal with them both, through this example. However, as the title asks you to consider "such conflicts", you will need to look for some **other examples** of where *two knowledge sources* seem to *conflict*.

Make claims and develop perspectives using authentic examples to illustrate and support your discussion

You might decide that, having watched the movie Pulp Fiction, you found many reasons for saying that the movie is good (AOK: the arts), but your emotional reactions to several scenes tell you that it is bad (WOK: emotion, and AOK: ethics). Then you might point out that "good" and "bad" can be used in an aesthetic sense or a moral sense, so the conflict is shown to be apparent through thinking about the WOK of language.

However, in the case of science it is commonly perceived that science attempts to develop theories that are true and objective. Scientific work is commonly viewed as involving observations and experimentation with natural phenomena, which become increasingly accurate and universalized over time. Is this true, or is science culturally bound?

Analyse and argue

Provide effective counterclaims, counter-arguments and counter-examples to support them.

You could argue that such apparent conflicts arise because facts are dependent upon context, such as the facts about the nature of the atom, which change according to changing theories.

You could provide other examples to show how it can ultimately be argued that facts are merely interpretations. This could develop into a postmodernist perspective that scientific theories are just as likely to be social constructs as works of art or cultural artifacts.

Can you think of an example of conflict between sources of knowledge that does not seem reconcilable?

Evaluate and conclude

Will you argue that all such apparent conflicts can be reconciled by realizing that they are each reasonable interpretations within their own frameworks and contexts?

Will you argue that some conflicts are real now, but are due to our inadequate knowledge at present?

Will you argue that there are real, unreconcilable conflicts in our knowledge?

This essay achieved 11/40, a grade D

A

The introduction does reflect on conflicts of knowledge, but only in a general way. The student does not show how these generalized knowledge conflicts relate to the specifics of the title. The final sentence is overstated.

It can be helpful to reflect broadly on the KIs in your introduction, but it is essential to make links between these reflections and the detailed wording of the essay title.

Conflicts in knowledge are prevalent in human nature and interaction. They can occur in a single person's mind. They can exist between individuals or between larger schools of thought. Knowledge conflicts have the power to initiate wars and inspire quests for enlightenment. The most convoluted dilemmas in the human process stem from incompatible results from different sources of knowledge. But do these conflicting results indicate conflicting truths? Recognizing the ability of different approaches to yield different results may not lead to reconciliation, but it may lead to a fuller understanding of truth and knowledge. Every person has preconceptions pertaining to what is possible and what is impossible, what is right and what is wrong. When one comes upon something previously thought impossible or wrong, one must choose how to process the new information. One can reject it altogether; incorporate it into one's predetermined view and justify it to fit the parameters of accepted possibility; or welcome it and allow it to change one's perspective. When an individual is presented with a conflict of knowledge, she or he must decide how to approach the conflict, and decide what is true for her- or himself. Because of infinite approaches, it is possible that infinite truths could be found in every situation.

> ## C
> The case here is overstated—how could there be an infinity of truths?
>
> Beware making exaggerated claims.

Internal conflicts are often the most difficult to reconcile, for one must step outside oneself to find a knowledgeable path that can justify both points of view. In the 2001 documentary <promises, filmmaker B.Z. Goldberg attempts to understand the effect of the Israeli-Palestinian conflict on children living in both Palestine and Israel, and foster understanding between them. Throughout the film, he becomes close to the children he is interviewing, and the children in turn come to love him. In one scene, Goldberg reveals to a young Palestinian boy, Mahmoud, that he is Jewish. Mahmoud is taken aback, for he has grown up learning to hate all Jewish people; his love for Goldberg goes against everything he has ever known. Mahmoud's rational mind tells him that he should hate Goldberg, but in his heart he knows that Goldberg is good. He is presented with an ethical and cultural dilemma. The internal conflict is especially difficult because Mahmoud cannot see the situation from another point of view. He is conflicted with himself, and only he can determine what is moral. In this case, Mahmoud chooses to accept that his relationship with Goldberg is moral, but he justifies it by insisting that Goldberg isn't truly Jewish. His method of determining truth is to mold this "impossibility" to fit the borders of his perspective. From Goldberg's perspective, however, their relationship is moral, even though Mahmoud's culture is in direct offense of Goldberg's identity. Thus each must compromise one knowledge result for another.

> ## B
> The student shows a personal approach in finding an example of conflict across cultural paradigms.
>
> Draw on your own experience, including the media, to find authentic, personally meaningful examples.

> ## A
> Although this example is noteworthy, the student does not make clear how it illustrates a conflict between two sources of knowledge. At least some prior discussion of that issue, probably through the table example, is necessary so that the reader can understand the underlying KI.
>
> Explain explicitly the connections between any example provided and the KIs implied by the title.

Some people, when confronted with unfamiliar or "impossible" situations, reject the new information altogether. The Pirahã tribe in northwestern Brazil has a collective culture that exists completely in the moment. This is reflected in their behavior, especially towards people who are foreign to their tribe, and their language. They have no sense of abstraction or pattern, no modern concept of past or future. Thus, when speaking of a person walking away and out of sight, a Piraha tribe member says that they have "gone out of existence." When the person returns, he or she has "come into existence." In the minds of the Pirahã, there is no concept of that which does not directly relate to them in the moment. Despite decades of contact with the outside

> ## C
> This example has potential, but it is purely descriptive. There is very little attempt to analyse it in relation to the title.
>
> Explain explicitly the connections between any example provided and the KIs implied by the title.

B

It is not clear how this example (of differing conventions) is relevant to the KI mentioned in the title (different sources of knowledge).

Concentrating on just one word of a title ("conflict") is unlikely to ensure that you understand the intent of the whole title.

D

This interesting example does, at least implicitly, concern two sources (WOK emotion and AOK ethics). The student does not, however, draw attention to its relevance.

A C

(Page 71)

The student concludes that relativism addresses the issues raised in the title. However, the examples they have provided have not supported an argument for this hypothesis. Showing that people do disagree does not demonstrate that they should. Neither does the discussion explore the title's suggestion that these conflicts might be reconcilable.

Do not make unsupported assumptions or jump to conclusions! Always ensure your analysis of the title and your argument in the body lead to your essay's final conclusion and evaluation.

world, they continue to reject every aspect of other cultures. Their approach to the unfamiliar is often mild but fleeting interest. When a plane arrives carrying people from outside the Amazon, a Piraha boy may create a detailed model of the machine. Soon after, however, the toy is abandoned. The plane, as an aspect of outside culture, is rejected and forgotten; the whole process will be repeated the next time a plane touches down near the village. Experiments performed on the tribe by sociologists and linguists have failed, for the Pirahã cannot grasp the concepts involved, nor do they understand the implications of the research. This knowledge conflict is unique in that it involves a discrepancy in necessity of knowledge between the Piraha and the researchers.

In some cases, two branches of the same area of knowledge can clash. For instance, the formula for internal energy change differs slightly depending on whether the observer approaches from a "chemistry viewpoint" or "physics viewpoint." When studying this concept in chemist's terms, the formula is written as $\Delta U = q + w$, in which "ΔU" represents internal energy change, "q" the energy produced by the system and "w" the work done on the system. However, when a physicist is asked to write the formula, he or she will likely generate the following: $\Delta U = q - w$. In this formula, "w" stands for the work done *by* the system. This seems a small change to someone who has never studied chemistry or physics, but when one contemplates this difference in scientific terms, one can see that it demonstrates a great and very important deviation in thought between the two fields. When a chemist studies a substance, such as a certain gas, he or she is interested most deeply in the internal functions of said substance. Therefore the chemist will compute "work" as any work done on the system and this affecting any intermolecular aspects such as bond behavior. However, a physicist will approach the problem with the view that work is being done by the system. This is because one of the fundamental focuses of physics—the increased efficiency of a system in the surrounding environment—is completely different from the more contained goal of chemistry.

Even humor can result in a contradiction of knowledge. When someone tells a racist joke, the audience is confronted with two conflicting truth issues: first, the appeal of humor and second, the morality of what is being said (in this case one must assume that the audience is against said racism). It is true that laughter is the natural reaction to wit, but it is also true that the audience knows that the joke is unethical by general societal standards. If the audience chooses to laugh at the joke, then they are sacrificing ethics in favor of humor. However, if the audience is affronted, then morality has triumphed over comedic entertainment. Different members of the same audience may be offended or entertained, so that the joke teller is actually a mediator of the knowledge conflict.

Ralph Waldo Emerson said, "One man's justice is another's injustice; one man's beauty another's ugliness; one man's wisdom another's folly." The examples presented in this paper demonstrate the relativistic quality of truth as it relates to conflicts in knowledge. Often times these conflicts cannot be reconciled because of the immense difference in approach. These conflicts do not, however, indicate conflicts of truth. Many different truths can be deduced from a single phenomenon if one approaches with many different ways of knowing. Every person sees the world with different eyes, and therefore must define for her- or himself how to define truth in every situation.

Word Count: 1239

D There are no references for the essay even though there are clearly examples that require acknowledgement for the sources of the information.

It is important that referencing should be provided and that it should permit tracing of the sources. This is for academic honesty and also in order that anyone interested in the topic and the related issues can follow them up and undertake their own investigation.

Examiner report

Criterion A: (3) There is very little treatment of **relevant** KIs. The student makes reference to some KIs, but they are not linked to the title. There are four explicit links to AOKs (media and arts, ethics, human sciences) but how the situations described relate to the type of conflict mentioned in the title is not made clear, even when the student considers the natural sciences, an AOK mentioned in the title.

Criterion B: (4) There is personal engagement and independent thinking, but it does not relate sufficiently to the title. The examples and ensuing perspectives are clear and quite well developed. However, they do not illustrate or allow exploration of the sort of conflict, described in the title, between results produced by different sources of knowledge, such as the WOK human senses and the AOK natural science (physics).

Criterion C: (2) Although the essay flows quite coherently, it does not develop an inquiry that addresses the KIs implied by the conflict presented in the title. The arguments are at times coherent enough in themselves, but generally irrelevant to the title. Some of the discussion is too descriptive. This does not make for a convincing inquiry.

Criterion D: (2) Although the essay is quite well structured, the ideas and arguments are often not relevant to the title. The information provided is not necessarily reliable, especially since there is no referencing of sources used.

Overall …

Although as the essay is quite well written and there are some interesting examples and discussion, it does not treat the knowledge issues relevant to the title. The title implied a need to explore the different approaches and paradigms used to acquire knowledge of the same phenomenon, a table, but the student never did this.

The essay has interesting material. The examples are described well but are not tied into an adequate framework of argument related to the prescribed title. The essay is short (only just over the minimum). What do you think went wrong here? What lessons can be learnt from it? We suspect the student may have run out of time: useful material was collected but the student was not able to reflect on it sufficiently to make it work effectively. Sometimes it helps to do some work on a topic, then leave it alone for a while and come back to it. You can do this only if you are well ahead of your deadline.

How would you advise the student to develop the essay better? How would you plan for this essay? How would you recommend breaking down the terms and knowledge conflicts indicated in the title in order to address them?

Finally, the student has not referenced the sources used. It's advisable to keep a record of sources as you write the essay in order that the references list can be a relatively straightforward task.

This essay achieved 22/40, a grade C

The student assumes that the reader understands what is meant by the terms "ways of knowing" (D) and "the senses", as well as by the title. These all need to be briefly explained.

In your introduction, always clarify the way you understand the title, as well as any TOK terms and concepts that you use.

The student identifies an assumption in the title.

When planning, check whether the title contains a questionable assumption. If so, question it.

The student clarifies ideas by using headings (D). This helps organize the ideas in order to clarify a main KI raised by the title (A).

Used appropriately, section headings can help clarify an essay's organization and thus help it to address KIs effectively.

The exploration here extends and personalizes the original table example; it examines the student's understanding of the table from a scientific perspective.

Personalizing a theoretical example shows your engagement in the KI.

Careful and detailed exploration of the example develops a counterclaim to the title's assumption.

There are several ways of knowing, and our senses is one of them. Yet our ways of knowing can be flawed, and sometimes they contradict each other. Such a scenario is the one described in the question for this essay: <<Our senses tell us that the table, for example, is a solid object; science tells us that the table is mostly empty space. Thus the two sources of knowledge generate conflicting results. Can we reconcile such conflicts? >>

The premise is flawed

The premise here seems to be that there is conflicting results. I want to contest that premise; there is not necessarily a conflict between the two sources of knowledge.

A natural scientists view: Why it does not generate conflicting results

First, let's look at what makes a table mostly empty space, and let us look at what actually happens when I touch a table, at an atomic level.

A table consists of different matter; of atoms and molecules. The atoms are consisting of electrons and the nucleus. Electrons are far away from the core, compared to the size of the core (this is what makes the atom mostly empty space). An atom will keep its distance to other atoms with its electro force which is generated by the electron. When another atom hits its electro field it will be repulsed by it and bounce away or in the very least not pass.

So, when I touch the table, the collective electric forces of the atoms in the table meet the electric forces in the atoms of my finger (or hand, or foot) and so my fingers are stopped from moving further in that direction.

At the tip of my fingers there are placed a special breed of cells named nerve cells. When they are subject to certain conditions, this is supposed to trigger a reaction in these cells and they send signals to my brain, telling me that something happens to them; in this case the signal they send is that they are subject to pressure.

According to the field of physics my nerve cells are supposed to undergo a certain amount of pressure when my fingers are pressed towards the table; according to biologists the nerve cells are then supposed to give me the sensation of <<solid object>> when exposed to such pressure. According to this perspective there is no conflicting

The student uses their own words to present a layperson's perspective through a hypothetical example that shows the sense perception view (B).

The student explains in careful detail (C).

Tailoring an explanation to the details of the title shows your personal reflection and integrates a knowledge perspective into your inquiry. Used skilfully, a hypothetical example can be effective, although generally they are best avoided.

The introduction of a third religious viewpoint neatly leads to a reinterpretation of the conflict as an issue of interpretation.

Consideration of different perspectives strengthens and adds depth to the quality of inquiry.

sources of knowledge; <<mostly empty space>> is supposed to give the sensation of <<solid object>>. When I feel a solid object such as a table I know it to be how <<mostly empty space>> feels like. If I was to come in contact with completely filled space this would be a black hole and the sensation would be that of my body being ripped apart. Therefore one can regard it as not being conflicting sources of knowledge.

The layman's perspective

People who are not as well versed in physics as the natural scientists may think differently. They may look at the table and observe that it appears whole and solid. It occupies a certain space in the room. When they touch it with their hands it doesn't yield to their hands like air, fog or water; and if they break it up, no matter how small the bits they break it down into and no matter where they look they would never (know how to) find a point where there is nothingness or where the table is porous.'

Then, when science tells him that the table is mostly empty space this might sound counter-intuitive. The reasoning behind it might be like this: The table feels solid. If something is solid, it likely must be made up from something solid. Ergo, the stuff which solid matter is made from must be solid. I have never seen something very very small and consisting of almost nothing which is solid, therefore empty space is not solid.

The importance of interpretation

The difference between the two accounts described above is the way they interpret their sensory input. To illustrate: Let's imagine a third person who touches the table. Let's assume this person has a religion or conviction which states that everything material is an illusion. Such a person will not regard the assertion that a table is mostly empty space as something shocking or conflicting, but rather as a confirmation of his world view.

1. Freudenrich, Craig. "How atoms work." Howstuffworks. 31 Jan 2008 <http://www.howstuffworks.comJatom.htm>.

2 KahI, Ulrika, "Signaling between Nerve Cells." Human brain institute. 31 Jan 2008 <http://www.hubin.org/facts/brain/texts/nervceIl_signaling_en.htm1>.

All sensory input must be interpreted in some way. We interpret things based on our experience and thoughts. And the more interpretation, the more knowledge we can gain. The sensation of touching a bottle is the same as the sensation of being touched by a bottle (assuming it is done using the same angle and force). How can we whether we hit it or are hit by it? We must find out that through

knowledge; if I know that I don't move I can't be the one who touched the bottle and not the opposite. The sensation can be interpreted further; for example it should be possible to derive from the touch what direction the bottle is from you. If it hits you in the foot with large speed you could derive that someone is playing the popular <<bottle football>> in the corridors at school (provided you are at school, and that there are no other reason why anyone should throw a bottle at you).

How to reconcile a conflict

What makes the two sources of knowledge conflict is the interpretation of the sensory input. One way to reconcile such conflicts is to find an interpretation which is more correct, possibly through discussion and study of the field, as I gave an example of previously in the text. Some would take the relativist approach and say that it is impossible to find a correct interpretation, and that two conflicting views may both be correct. In such case reality would be dependent on the viewer.

One good way to reconcile such a conflict would be to try to find contradictions in your sensory input. Say, for example, that you see a Ponzo illusion

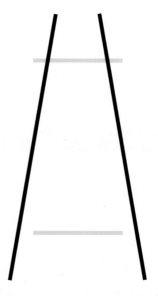

The bottle example, being both hypothetical and too general, does not assist the argument well.

Real-life or authentic examples discussed in detail are far more effective in providing justification.

This paragraph is helpful since the student summarizes the central claims that have been made about interpretation and the relativity of knowledge in the previous paragraphs. Structurally, the paragraph helps the clarification and organization of ideas.

The writer presents two alternative views without an attempt to come to a decision.

Pointing out alternative views is good, but it is necessary to offer a critical appraisal of them.

The Ponzo illusion example could be clearer. Is it an argument against the relativist approach?

Clearly spell out the implications of your examples. If you don't they do not demonstrate any perspective or approach clearly.

D B

The Ponzo illusion example could be clearer. Is it an argument against the relativist approach?

Clearly spell out the implications of your examples. If you don't they do not demonstrate any perspective or approach clearly.

A

This conclusion is very brief, offering little overview of the discussion, nor much evaluation of the original KI.

Use your conclusion to briefly recap on the arguments, and to provide some brief but insightful evaluation of the KIs.

Most people think the upper yellow line is larger than the lower, even though they are equally large. In order to find out which is correct, you could use other ways of knowing such as measuring it with a ruler—when you find a contradiction between what your eyes tell you and what the ruler tells you know that one is incorrect (unless you believe both to be correct). Personally the knowledge that the two lines are equally large makes me able to look at the picture in another way,

But how can you know which of the ways of knowing is right, when the two gives conflicting views? Determining which the correct one is can usually be done through more investigation using other ways of knowing to find out. Note that in such a case the conflict is not reconciled, but one of the sources of knowledge is proven to be wrong in this case. Or, maybe you'll find a better way to interpret the knowledge gained.

Conclusion

If you gain conflicting knowledge from different sources of knowledge, it may be a good idea to investigate it further, so that you can find a better interpretation of the knowledge gained. In such a case you can know how to reconcile the knowledge.

Word count: 1229

! Examiner report

Criterion A: (5) Although the student addresses KIs (flawed premise, conflict of approaches) relevant to the title, these issues are explored only in a limited fashion. KIs are not considered in a wider context, but mainly limited to perception and physics. The student does briefly consider religion, but does not sufficiently develop a line of reflection in order to achieve a genuine breadth of understanding. A good start is thus undermined by a failure to explore sufficiently the broader applications.

Criterion B: (6) The student's approach to the title is quite original, showing some degree of independent thinking. Personal reflection is evident in some of the examples considered (awareness of atoms in the table, a layman's view, hitting the bottle). However, there the student demonstrates little awareness

that perspectives exist outside the ones explicitly suggested by the title.

Criterion C: (5) The student uses claims and examples quite skillfully in order to generate critical inquiry. A successful counterclaim to the "conflict" hypothesis is provided, suggesting that apparent conflict masks compatibility when considered from an alternative viewpoint. However, the argument is not sufficiently developed; the inquiry therefore remains satisfactory but somewhat limited.

Criterion D: (6) The student structures the essay and organizes ideas quite effectively, using headings and synopses to provide clarification of issues and arguments. On the other hand, at the start of the essay some terms and concepts are left unexplained where the student could have provided definitions. Although there is

some referencing of sources, it is by no means complete.

Overall …

This essay just achieved a satisfactory high C because the student certainly addresses KIs and develops argumentation. However, specific improvements could be made to the essay. They include the clarification of concepts in the introduction and a more complete referencing of sources used. Do you think that student could have also achieved more marks and thus a B rather than a C if they had carried over the arguments into a wider variety of situations and contexts? How do you think this could have been done in order to gain a wider range of perspectives and a greater breadth of understanding of the KIs?

A The student presents and explores differing perspectives or worldviews, ie a traditional Eastern and a modern Western cultural understanding of "energy". The discussion relates well to the title and is very successful in developing inquiry into the KI.

C By including counter-views, the student opens opportunities to achieve a level of analytic detail. There is a resulting sense of more depth in the essay's inquiry into the KIs.

Acknowledge, and deal fairly with, perspectives which clash with even your most cherished beliefs.

B The extract shows personal engagement through a fresh, original approach and thus independent thinking about the KIs. The cultural aspect is genuine and explained from the inside. Self-awareness as a knower is particularly well developed in the examples of Chi in practice.

Personal examples can contain a depth of understanding and feeling that makes the discussion all the more compelling.

C This claim certainly needs a reference.

All facts need to be referenced, unless they are general knowledge.

Chi is everything and everywhere. It is the universal force that keeps us alive and also keeps the universe together. In art or medicine, philosophy or martial arts, Chi is ingrained in virtually every aspect of Asian culture, especially that of China. I was taught Chinese Calligraphy by my grandfather when I was really young, and still practice this ancient form of art and meditation. In Calligraphy, Chi is imperative. I was taught to invite the Chi of the earth into my body through my feet, then mixing it with my own Chi, guide it through my body to the tip of my hand that is holding the brush. With will power and concentration, I should push the Chi from the tip of the brush and pierce through the paper. It is a very exhausting practice, but I feel myself strengthened from the movement of my Chi after every word I write. Yet, I never once denounced the people who believed that there was no such thing as Chi. I adopted a mentality from my grandfather which asks myself why they deny what I know to be true. Maybe they see it as something else or maybe they were meant to sense it yet. Whatever the case, in time, when they are ready, science will show then Chi.

Chi is accepted as true by a large percentage of the world's population. However, in the not too distant past, science was not able to detect Chi with any instruments. Nor was JingLui, the network through which Chi was supposed to travel, never discovered during any autopsy. Thus Chi, for the longest time, was seen as a superstition or pseudoscience. I am sure of its existence. I can feel it surge through my body when I practice Calligraphy, I can feel it move around me as I manipulate it during Tai Chi. And after I meditate for a period of time and then slowly move my hands closer and closer together, I can feel a force resisting and pushing my hands away from each other. Yet mainstream science deemed it as a mere myth. Chi was there, that's the truth seen by the Chinese for 5000 years. The scientists couldn't see it because the source of knowledge was not advanced enough to perceive Chi. But contemporary science is able to detect an energy field around humans called the bioenergetic field that fits the description of thousands of years of Chinese culture. The field is strong enough along the places where the main Jing Luis were said to be and can be altered by people who have command of the Chi. Tradition has pointed out that Chi was there, a fact that science was not yet ready to see. But with patience and tolerance, the believers of Chi gave the practitioners of science enough time to develop instruments sensitive enough to detect Chi and to realize that they were looking at Chi this whole time.

This essay achieved 38/40, a grade A

B A

The student introduces the essay in a very individual manner, showing fine self-awareness as a knower. This lively, interactive example invites the reader to experience the same situation. It explores a perspective implied by the title and later draws links with the student's IB studies. All this allows the KI raised in the prescribed title to be revealed vividly.

Try to engage the reader when introducing KIs and contested concepts. Examples of authentic situations and references to your IB studies make KIs more relevant, accessible and personal.

C

After expanding the initial example in terms of the title, the student introduces a counterclaim. Thus, the implications of the examples can be considered further, providing insights into more subtle aspects of the KI.

Use counterclaims in a detailed and critical manner to develop new and different perspectives, rather than simply providing a "con" claim to a previous "pro" one.

D

Throughout the essay, the student provides excellent "signposts" to make the line of argument clear, as in this paragraph, by linking back to the title's original example or using topic sentences to introduce the subject of paragraph.

B

Despite some confusion about Ramanujan summation, this mathematical example effectively supports the contrast of abstract and empirical reasoning through skilful development of the detail.

Stick a finger above your head. Do you feel the air surrounding us? Whereas scientific knowledge suggests that nitrogen, oxygen, and innumerous other particles surround our atmosphere, it sounds absurd one can empirically sense something that cannot be seen, heard, smelt, felt, or tasted. Then how do we know air exists at all? Now wet your finger, and swing it around a little. Or simply step outside for a second and try the dorky exercise again. The coolness sensed by your fingertip may not be air itself, but certainly enough to be assured that you will not suffocate by the sudden epiphany: that what you breathe in everyday does not actually exist. What one senses in this case is the *movement* of air. Try fanning your ear this time. Hear the wind? Wait until dinner time and you will notice that you can in fact smell air as well, or arrive at the more logical conclusion that smell itself is a phenomenon due to air.

The conclusion to this home-made experiment is not "sure, air exists," however. The intended lesson here is to realize the limitations of human perception and that in order to understand empirically that air exists we must *feel* its movement. Or, we can vicariously follow our predecessors' thoughts and learn that air consists of 78% nitrogen, 21% oxygen, and 1% of various other gas particles. (Tarbuck 325) This discrepancy between our dry and insensitive fingertips -that feels, well, nothing- and "the Atmosphere" chapter of a typical environmental systems textbook extends to the presumption that two sources of knowledge "conflict." Whereas in the example above there is one prevailing result over another -that in fact air does exist-, however, this is not always the case. Our four ways of knowing, namely perception, logic, emotion, and language, do not demand a choice. It is the predilection of ours to empirically feel an entity before believing its existence, or our innate obstinacy that makes us crave the visual in order to understand a concept which gives an illusion of "conflict." Thus we cannot accept that a table is mostly empty space without seeing or feeling the emptiness: an irony in itself. In fact, a table is both empty space and a solid object; scientific observations, involving microscopic studies of particles show that the table is mostly empty space, whereas our limited perception only feels solidity.

Two main sources of knowledge that seemingly confront each other are the empirical and the abstract. Consider the Ramanujan Sum. Mathematical derivation, known as proof, suggests that $1+2+3+\ldots$ to infinity converges to $-1/12$. Our empirical knowledge, which also leads to "common sense" tell us *no*, place a dollar, add another two dollars, add another three… if continual accumulation leads to a deficit, Bill Gates is not going to last long. But then again, Bill Gates is not going to live forever; no one has, and never will, reach infinity by definition. The sum cannot be seen, felt, heard, smelt, or tasted—never empirically tested. The human limitation here is our mortality, which causes utter confusion when attempting to grasp the meaning of infinity. This can be perhaps more easily illustrated by one of David Hilbert's renowned 23 problems. Let us assume there is a hotel that has an infinite number of rooms, in which, thanks to the seasonal rush, is occupied fully by an infinite number of guests. But alas, another group of infinite tourists arrive, demanding a set of infinite rooms. Our common sense, constructed through our empirical perception of the world, immediately visualizes a full house and dismisses the possibility that another infinite number of guests can fit. What the genius hotelier Hilbert does is ask all guests who do have a room to move to the room number double their current room number. Hence the guest in room 1 moves to room 2, the guest in room 2 moves to room 4, the guest in room 3 to room 6… so on so forth. What happens, in effect, is that the original guests now occupy only the even numbered rooms. Then the new group of infinite guests can occupy the odd numbered rooms (1, 3, 5, 7…). Because Hilbert strictly separates the empirical from the abstract and at the same time acknowledges that there is a difference—not conflict—between an empirical solution and a mathematical one, he is able to "reconcile" the apparent impossibility. The same can be applied for the Ramanujan sum, in that it is unnecessary—and impossible—to comprehend infinity within our finite life spans, and a mental set that denies something unseen is what prevents us from admitting its logical legibility. Therefore, the only way to reconcile the conflict hereby is to acknowledge there is not one.

Often even an empirically observable entity can result in a so-called conflict. Light, explained in one way, must be a bundle of photons, discrete particles that travel linearly. Yet in other experimental studies, light acts as a wave, frequently overlapping or even cancelling each other. This interdisciplinary conflict cannot be as easily resolved by the thought process delineated above, since this contradiction is a practical one and cannot be solved by advanced theoretical thinking. However, one is still bound to the limits of visualization if he/she cannot make sense of two apparently—and only apparently—opposing results. Light may be a wave, may be a particle, and may be both or neither. It is like a false dilemma squared. We must recognize that the attempt to define

---

D The student provides clarity with a clearly stated claim that introduces a new area to the essay's discussion.

Optimize your use of paragraphing to organize your ideas and to further your argumentation.

A B C The student shows how the apparently conflicting models available to explain light can be reconciled. This shows a subtle understanding of the role of models in the AOK of natural sciences (B,C). The examples further discussion of KIs relating to the "conflict" raised in the title (A).

An example can simultaneously satisfy several criteria at once, such as treatment of KIs (A) through exploration of perspectives (B) and detailed analysis (C).

light's behavior in terms of waves or particles is restrictive already, visualizing an entity to our convenience. And while for all practical uses either explanation works for a specific task, it is again impossible to forcefully converge the two theories into one comprehensive whole. We cannot see the particles of light scattering about or strings of light oscillating as if a sine curve, and when considered to greater depth, it is light itself that allows us to see in the first place. Explanations of light in a certain model, therefore, are in effect metaphors of something that is empirically unobservable. In other words, theories of light are aid to our human limitations in order to understand its properties, not absolute truth in itself. In some cases, such a model may develop to encompass all possibilities known, as in the case of atoms. Throughout the last hundred years of nuclear physics, the "correct model" for the atom has changed from the Rutherford model, through the Bohr model to the Schrodinger model, finally embracing most phenomena without conflict. Yet again when another property of the atom is revealed, the newest model may become, once again, history. In order to understand how a scientific fact can be altered within decades or even days, we must realize such "facts" are named "theories" and "models," merely tools to fit our convenience.

In other cases, there are distinct interpretations among disciplines considering one subject. Upon asking the meaning of "love" to a panel of teachers, I received from the biology teacher "an instinctive effort of gene preservation;" from the psychology teacher, "the continual quest for finding the ideal counterpart under Jungian archetypes of the other sex;" from the math teacher a friendly advice not to take a tape measurer on a first date and from the theatre teacher, "I can't even start or end" ("Theory of Knowledge: classroom discussion"). These discrepancies in interpretation—and advice—too, are various attempts to formulate an intangible concept. Numerous love songs, from those lamenting an unattained romance to those reeking with chemicals seem testimony to this disparity of interpretation. And at times, this emotional response (love) goes against your own logical reasoning. Your palms may sweat, your knees shake and pulse race at the mere sight of that figure across a crowded room, but logic (and maybe even your parents) might suggest what a lousy match this is, that in fact, it defies all logic. You like to travel, she is a homebody; you reach for the vegetarian menu while he stuffs his face with a triple whopper… And yet again the intangible force of attraction, beyond comprehension and most certainly out of the visual realm (unless demonstrated of course) bonds Romeo and Juliet, Tristan and Isolde to an extent that they risk their lives for

---

D

This introductory claim could be clearer: it obscures the meaning of an interesting paragraph.

Reread your essay for clarity (and ask someone else to), then edit accordingly.

A B

This personal "mini survey" of opinions works well to highlight the different approaches of AOKs, which are then explored.

Draw on your experience for authentic examples, and make sure you analyse their implications.

D

The contrast of the variety of interpretations for an intangible concept (love) sharpens aspects of the KI explored previously.

B C

An entertaining, well-written example (B) brings life to a quite solid theoretical analysis of the difference between scientific and emotional approaches (C).

Appropriate use of humour and wit can liven up your essay while strengthening critical discussion.

Very careful critical analysis (C), including contrasts of differing perspectives, leads to a highly personal (B) account of further subtle aspects of the KI (A).

Though brief, the conclusion addresses the central KI raised by the title in a clear and firm manner. Excellent summation of the line of argument throughout the body of the essay means this is sufficient.

Your conclusion should reflectively evaluate and offer final comments upon the central KIs.

Although sources are referenced, they should be in alphabetical order. Some other factual claims should have been referenced.

love. Here emerges another conflict that these lovers give up genetic preservation for love, which, according to the biological perspective, is the very definition of this life-threatening, reckless infatuation. For this particular predicament, there is no absolute answer, nor can it be attributed to a perceptual issue that because we cannot see love, we create a model for it. While it is a valid claim that love, as an abstract concept such as infinity or an intangible entity such as air requires observable phenomena to know its existence, laws and models seem to vary for every individual and every case within the person as well. Love, whether romance or lust, whether a primitive pursuit for gene preservation or platonic benevolence, pertains to emotional knowledge -something we know intuitively, or rather, feel without even knowing. As relativistic as it may sound, love means something different for everyone. Thus reconciling between conflicting explanations of love is not a logical choice in the field of philosophy, but an intuitive—and often instinctive—merging of knowledge.

Essentially, most scientific theories are extended metaphors, to make sense of a world beyond human comprehension in our own terms. Whether limited because the universe is unobservable in certain realms by us, restrained by our very effort to create a holistic model of nature, or dependent on inherent human nature indefinable by logic, there is no conflict to reconcile here—merely our restricted paradigm and an obsession to know all.

Works Cited

Tarbuck, Edward, J. Earth Science. 10. New York: Prentice Hall, 2005.

Gurney, Tim. "Theory of Knowledge: classroom discussion." American School of The Hague, Wassenaar, The Netherlands. 15 10 2007

Wenger, Ann. "Theory of Knowledge: classroom discussion." American School of The Hague, Wassenaar, The Netherlands. 15 10 2007

Faber, John. "Theory of Knowledge: classroom discussion." American School of The Hague, Wassenaar, The Netherlands. 15 10 2007

Cunningham, Anthony. "Theory of Knowledge: classroom discussion." American School of The Hague, Wassenaar, The Netherlands. 15 10 2007

Word count: 1599

Examiner report

Criterion A: (9) The essay develops a focused and sophisticated understanding of the KIs relevant to the title. Just as the title introduces the KI of conflicting knowledge, so the student tends to use examples (Ramanujan's mathematics, the hotel rooms) in order to address the KIs. The student also uses perspectives (empirical, abstract) as a means of exploring the KIs. The concepts of a metaphor and "our human" paradigm are offered to provide a conclusive evaluation of the knowledge conflicts.

Criterion B: (10) Right from the vivid immediacy of the example in the introduction (perception of air), the student has shaped the essay in a way that shows engagement with KIs. There is also a strong awareness of perspectives associated with examples (light, love), which the student shows are connected to theories that can be reconciled once it is acknowledged that these theories are simply metaphors to help human understanding of what cannot be observed.

Criterion C: (10) The student uses counter-examples and critical analysis as vehicles through which to develop different perspectives and to reveal further subtle aspects regarding the KIs. There is in-depth inquiry concerning the underlying theme throughout the essay of knowledge being founded upon models and interpretation.

Criterion D: (9) Ideas are very well organized in the essay thanks to the student's use of introductory and conclusive statements to paragraphs, thus providing clarity and cohesion to ideas and arguments. The use of language and style throughout the essay vividly and effectively develops and transmits the arguments and analysis in a compelling manner that makes the essay's inquiry so effective. Referencing of sources could have been more complete and alphabetical order was not used.

Overall …

This essay shows evidence of very independent thinking with serious and well-developed consideration of the KIs raised by the title. How do you think the student's vivid approach and well-explained examples help achieve this? In what way do the examples and the discussion of them contribute to the depth and breadth of the inquiry? How will you plan your essay to show similar qualities?

This extract was taken from an essay that achieved 36/40, a grade A (A = 9, B = 9, C = 9, D = 9).

This extract develops an analysis of the KI by considering another WOK—language—in relation to the WOK sense perception and AOK natural science mentioned in the title. It highlights the idea that one WOK can be limited by another. Essays can miss marks by taking a focus that is narrow, with limited consideration of AOKs and WOKs.

Greater insight can be gained into the KI raised by an essay title through exploring the relationship of named WOKs or AOKs to those not mentioned in the title.

This is not to say knowing that the table is mostly empty space, is not important. Knowing that a solid table is made up of billions of electrons, orbiting a nucleus of protons and neutrons, which creates empty space between the electrons and the nucleus, helps us to understand what the word "solid" means. By realizing that what we perceive as solid is actually made up of electrons, protons and neutrons, as are liquids and gases, we become aware of the interconnectedness of matter. We realize the "solid" table is only solid to our senses. This situation makes us uncertain as to what solid is. This uncertainty shows us we cannot only rely on one way of knowing to lead us to certainty on a subject. But while we may be uncertain about what a "solid" is, we are certain the table will always behave as a solid, which is what applies to our daily lives.

A language issue can be found at the root of this conflict; the issue being the words "solid" and "empty". Webster's dictionary defines a solid as being "filled with matter throughout; not hollow." Webster's

The extract shows careful exploration through the diverse perspectives of two different WOKs. The detail of the discussion contributes to the quality of inquiry into the KIs that the title raises.

Explore conflicting knowledge claims through different perspectives to achieve more detail and depth in your inquiry.

dictionary defines empty as "containing nothing; having nothing in it." These definitions contradict each other. We become uncertain because reason tells us something filled with matter cannot also be containing nothing. The words "filled" and "nothing" limit our understanding. Words also limit the scientist's ability to communicate what the empty space means. Referring back to the configuration of a solid being mostly empty space, helps us to understand what the word solid actually entails.

Kit 5

"Context is all" (Margaret Atwood). Does this mean that there is no such thing as truth?

[Title 10, from November 2007/May 2008]

Essay type

A type 1 title that emphasizes two TOK terms (context, truth), asking for evaluation across AOKs and/or WOKs (your choice).

Key words and phrases:

- Context, all, does this mean, no such thing, truth

Contestable concepts

- Context, truth

What do you understand by context? By truth? How are they related? Can you give a single account of each, or does their meaning shift in different AOKs?

Ambiguous phrases

- Context is all

What do you think "context is all" means?

Note: For titles that contain a quote, such as here, you do not have to research what Margaret Atwood was thinking when she said it. Your job is to give your own interpretation of the phrase, which you can explain and defend.

Does this mean you are going to take Margaret Atwood's quote out of context?

Action terms

- Does this mean, no such thing.

  You are being asked to make, and justify, a judgment about whether—if context is, indeed, all—it follows that truth does not exist.

Assumptions in the title

- That context **is** all.

Are you going to question whether context is all, or are you going to accept it?

- That the relationship between context and truth can be determined independently of the area of inquiry.

Are you going to argue that there are different relationships between context and truth in different AOKs?

Rephrase the title to check your understanding

Having thought about all the above, now is the time for you to make sure you understand the intent of the whole title. Here is one attempt at rephrasing:

- In deciding whether we can believe a knowledge claim, we need to know all about the claim, all related claims, the person making the claim and the environment in which the claim is made. Does this mean that we can never agree that any knowledge claim always holds?

This is just one way the question could be rewritten. It relies on an understanding of context that has four elements, and of truth as depending on agreement. Your unpacking of these two terms may be different from this.

Identify knowledge issues

Having clarified to your own satisfaction what the title is asking, you should now be able to identify the knowledge issue that you will target in your essay. Based on the above rewriting of the title, we might come up with several:

- If we always need to know all about the particular context (where, when, in what surroundings and by whom a knowledge claim is made), does this mean we can never all agree to the truth of that claim?

- If truth implies some form of objectivity, and our experience is always within a context—and hence subjective—how (if at all) can our experience lead to truth?

- Are the implications for truth of the claim that context is all dependent on the *theory of truth* we use, ie truth by *correspondence*, truth by *coherence* or *pragmatic* truth?

Brainstorming

Consider WOKs and AOKs

Since this title does not specifically mention any of the AOKs or WOKs, or the features of the knower and their communities, you will have to decide which ones you will deal with in your answer.

Do the knowledge claims in any of the AOKs seem to be particularly affected by context? Do any seem to be quite insensitive to context? Are there any that are not clear cut?

You might decide that claims about what is good music seem to depend on many contextual factors, such as the age of the knower, their culture, the time in history and so on. So you might choose the arts as one of your AOKs.

On the other hand, you might believe that the validity of a mathematical theorem depends on none of these factors, so you may choose mathematics as another AOK.

You may believe that historical claims can seem to depend on context, but might be able to be decided by careful attention to the evidence.

Which of the WOKs contribute to the arts' sensitivity to context? Which contribute to the non-reliance of mathematics on context? Here, you might explore the role of emotion and of language in the arts, and of reason in mathematics—and show why each affects that AOK's sensitivity to context.

Make claims and develop perspectives using authentic examples to illustrate and support your discussion

In a piece of music, a poem or a sculpture, how does emotion—through the mood, tone and associations—conjure up cultural context that could be relevant to the value of that piece of art? How can we judge whether a piece of art is "good" or "bad"? Does it depend upon who makes that judgment? Which music/poem etc will you use to illustrate this?

Considering language, in literature, how do aspects of language such as homophones and connotations engender context? What examples of homophones or connotations will you use?

Are there ways in which mathematics can be culturally context-related, such as number systems that differ from one society or era to another, for example Roman and Aztec numerals?

Analyse and argue

Provide effective counterclaims, counter-arguments and counter-examples to support them.

Can you think of contextual situations that are also to be viewed as universal? Language, viewed above as contextual, can also be cited as one of the major tools of globalization, for example advertising or the spread of English as a global language.

What aspects of mathematics or the natural sciences depend upon principles of objectivity and universality?

Evaluate and conclude

The title could be seen as implying that context and truth are mutually exclusive, but could you argue that this is not the case?

Could it be that, because of context, although some truths may be universal, their interpretation could change according to time or place?

Is some sort of context essential for truth—or for finding it? If you remove context, do you remove the possibility of meaningful truth?

Or is truth essentially about objectivity and public accountability that can be applied in a universal manner to any context, for example universal human rights or the value of eradicating disease through medical science?

This essay achieved 14/40, a grade D

D C

The student starts by considering key concepts: truth and then context. However "agreed truth" is not the account of truth used throughout the essay. He does not discuss objections to this account (D) or analyse the list of issues mentioned (C).

Ensure that the introduction sets up how you are going to use key terms, that your account is well supported and subsequently used and analysed consistently. Plan well to help develop a truly critical essay!

D A

This account needs to be expanded and supported. A confusion here between "relative truth" and "belief" becomes more apparent later (D). This major misconception runs throughout the essay (A).

Keep major TOK concepts clearly distinguished, particularly when it comes to truth, knowledge and belief.

C D

The argument is unsound: the conclusion does not follow from the premises. The [later] usage of "perceive" is unclear. Is this a reference to the WOK sense perception? And how is perception linked to truth?

Check that you claim no more from an argument than it can show. Use "perception" only to mean sense perception.

D C

The student slips from using "true" to "considered true" (ie "believed"), so the argument does not work. He then says "we discover more accurate explanations", contradicting the argument for relativity (C). Facts about myths not referenced (D)!

Consider carefully the implications of the words you choose (C). Factual claims must be referenced, unless common knowledge (D).

Truth can be defined in many different ways. In fact, I read that there are many theories made in the past that attempt to explain truth. Personally, I think truth is something that people agree on as right or correct even if it cannot be proven practical in real life. Different theories have different ways of understanding the concept of truth. This makes it difficult to decide whether or not truth exists. Three of the main theories of truth are Correspondence, Constructivist and Consensus[1]. Each theory has its own claims on what establishes truth. Theorists discuss two types of truth: relative and absolute. Personally, I believe that only relative truth exists, the one that contains context.

Context originates from our different age, desires, degree of experiences, beliefs, genders and the time periods in which we live. In order to find the difference between relative truths you have to know the whole concept behind them, the exact factors that affect them, and how they were created. Because of this, no such thing as absolute truth exists. On the other hand, truth can be shared at different levels according to reference frames. It can be individual, global, national, local, personal, religious, and racist. In other words, I believe that we perceive things based of our different cultural, religious, linguistic, social and technological backgrounds.

Mythology is one example on how truth changes with time and, therefore, cannot be considered as absolute. One of the myths that was considered true in the past is the belief of certain ancient people that the Sun was the God of light and fire. Another myth that people once believed is stated that the phenomenon of rain was actually God pouring out of an enormous cup. A myth in general shows how an idea can be seen as true until time passes and more information is gained, leading to newer theories and more conclusive ideas. Hence, we discover more accurate explanations for what happens in nature, which replace the old, initial, and basic ones that the early humans believed in due to their lack of cognitive abilities. As time passes, truth changes. Some people argue that there is absolute truth. When one says, "The light is on", he might consider it as absolute truth because the light really is on. However, we

---

1 http://en.wikipedia.org/wiki/Truth accessed online on October 21, 2007

C The student introduces critique, mentioning a counterclaim ("the light is on"), but does not extend it in order to develop a truly analytical argument.

Use counterclaims to test your main claims.

B The flat earth is an extremely clichéd example. A better one might be drawn from the author's Group 4 studies.

Choose fresh examples: often this is best done by drawing on your own experience.

D The student continues to confuse truth and belief (also opinion), which makes it difficult to follow the argument.

A This is the only place where the introduction's idea that "true" can be understood as "consensual" is used: elsewhere, truth is seen as relative to individuals.

Check what ideas you have introduced and follow up each one in order to be consistent.

D The text is very unclear and confused here.

Edit your essay for clarity.

have to take into consideration that the concept of light being on or off is based on a definition invented by humans. If a definition is invented by humans, we cannot really call it absolute truth. Another way to show that this is relative truth is by citing the example of a blind person, who because of his reference frame perceives the light as always off. Here we are talking about relative truth again.

At the same time, the truth changes even in science. The theories regarding the shape of the Earth are an example of how scientific truth keeps changing with time. At the beginning, people thought the Earth was flat; however, after further scientific research they realized that the Earth is actually spherical. Afterwards, when satellite images of the Earth were taken from outer space, people discovered that the Earth is an oblate spheroid, which holds true up to our day. This relative truth because it is based on human interpretation, which is influenced by knowledge and perceptions, it can only be considered as a relative one.

When I was a child, I used to think that God lives between the clouds and eats his meals while sitting on one of them. However, when I grew up I realized that it is just a simple thought that I don't really believe in anymore. Another simple thought I had in mind was that there is a big fan responsible for generating the wind on Earth. This proves that degree of experience is a factor in what you consider true and what you consider false. Thus, we cannot say that there is an absolute truth. If we say so, then we imply that each of us hold the same beliefs. This would mean that the other children also believed what I did about the world around me. In addition, this statement would also imply that my parents held the same opinion I did when I was a child. Wouldn't this also mean that my belief should not change with time? The common knowledge we have about the world that originates from our experience shows that this is not the case.

The theories we think of today as truths are invented by humans. When people agree on something, it usually becomes common knowledge. Time is such an example. In the past ancient people decided that a year consists of twelve months, that a month usually has thirty days, and so on. As a result they made a sequence that defines time and ways of measuring it. Nowadays, we regard time as absolute truth. One of the reasons is that none of us can decide to have their own measurement of time. However, there is a question of how "true" this measurement actually is. Time is not really an absolute truth; it is considered to be an absolute because we do not have any other alternatives to believe in.

(A)(B) The example the student gives here is barely science. It shows little understanding of the AOK natural science and its relation to truth.

Use strong, central examples from the AOK to show your grasp of their TOK implications.

(C) The student uses this counterclaim well, given the essay's major misconception: confusing truth with belief.

Counterclaims are effective means for testing arguments.

(B) The student offers personal comments that show little in the way of relevant independent thought, or deep reflection.

Putting a personal stamp on your essay needs to be more than merely stating your own opinion.

Natural sciences are some of the areas of knowledge with a similar problem. For example, I keep wondering who decided that the map of the Earth should be in the shape we all know. Why wouldn't it be drawn up side down? Because the knowledge about the map we have is limited by what scientists tell us, we all see the map as a correct one therefore, we think that it should be drawn in that way. But this proves that we cannot consider the map as absolute truth. The map is again, invented by humans.

Truth can vary according to religion. Different religions have different beliefs and ways of thinking. In Islam we have many beliefs that do not agree with what Christians believe. Christians believe that Jesus was killed the day after the Last Supper. However, in Islam we believe that he was saved and he ascended to the heavens. At the same time we believe the person who was planning to kill Jesus was the one who was crucified. Here religion shows us that there is no such thing as absolute truth. One could say that an absolute truth is that a divine entity exists because it is common to most religions. However, how do we prove that there is a higher power if we don't believe in any of the religions, in other words if we are atheists? At the same time "God" could be defined in many different ways according to the different reference frames in religions. Again in all depends on the beliefs that we as humans hold. This means that the truth in religion is considered to be a relative truth.

Famous philosophers spent a lot of time thinking and arguing about truth and how absolute it could be. However, I think what we believe to be the truth is usually related to how we perceive the world. We could have an individual, global, national, local, personal, religious and racist basis for how to judge and/or decide our relative truth. As a result there is no absolute truth. The statement "context is all" supports my argument. After deep thinking about this subject, I am strongly convinced that relative truth originates from our different perceptions.

[Word count: 1244]

Examiner report

Criterion A: (4) The student's understanding of the central KI for this title is weak, springing from a failure to distinguish between *truth* and *belief* (and also *meaning* and *knowledge*). While there are paragraphs on a number of AOKs (mainly science and religion) and passing references to WOKs (language, sense perception), the discussions show little understanding of these areas in depth. *Context* is mentioned several times, and a list of the features that contribute to it are given, but again there is little analysis to show depth of understanding.

Criterion B: (4) The student shows some evidence of independent thinking, but it is largely misconceived, therefore of limited relevance, and shows relatively little sign of reflection (despite the claim in the final sentence). A limited range of perspectives are considered. In particular, while there are mentions of the opposing view that truth is absolute, this is not developed or

critiqued. The examples chosen tend to be clichéd or very simple and, while they are sometimes used reasonably effectively within the confines of the essay's argument, they do not demonstrate much personal engagement.

Criterion C: (3) The essay is too descriptive, containing too little argument, analysis or evaluation. Some of the arguments used are unsound: they do not establish the conclusions claimed. A couple of counterclaims are mentioned, but not fully questioned and explored. The student seems to be unaware of the assumptions they have made and fails to consider the implications of their argument.

Criterion D: (3) The major flaw in this essay stems from the failure to give clear and coherent accounts of the key concepts from the title: *context* and, particularly, *truth*. The structure is episodic and not well organized: both science and religion

are considered twice, some paragraphs apart. The writing is usually reasonably clear, but there are passages that are difficult to follow. None of the factual claims are referenced.

Overall …

The essay is consistently undermined by a major conceptual flaw: the failure to keep the concepts of *truth* and *belief* separate. Such concepts are central to TOK, and it is vital to think them through clearly. The main argument of the essay is the flawed one that, since beliefs are individual, truth must be relative. What definitions of truth would you explore to answer the title? Could you argue that truth is nothing more than belief (and hence relative to individuals) and if so, how could you present this case? How would you improve the structure and the quality of the argument of this essay?

This extract was taken from an essay that achieved 7/40, a grade E (A = 2; B = 1; C = 3; D = 1).

D This selection from the introduction does not explain how the author understands the concept of either context or truth, even though both terms are mentioned.

Make it clear to your reader what you understand by the key terms of the title.

A It is difficult to see how parts of this introduction relate to the title, or to a KI drawn from the title.

Use the early part of your essay to identify the KI from the title and to make clear what the connection between your approach and the title/ KI is.

When evaluating a quote from Margaret Atwood that reads "Context is All,", it can be determined that the type of language asserted into a young developing mind can address the future context of the situations. Limiting the language used or the population that gets to use the language hinders the same future context in the situation. If it is possible to alter the amount of information that the developing mind is receiving, then it can also be said that it is possible to alter the truth of the future. …

In a society were it is the norm for the media authorities to withhold information from the general public, it is very easy to direct the attention towards things that focus the whole society in one particular direction. But the nature of this issue is that it detracts from other knowledge issues, such as ones that can be gathered from language,

A

The WOKs (and later the AOK ethics) are dropped into this essay with no attempt to explain how they are working or what their relevance is.

Merely mentioning TOK terms is not sufficient. You need to closely analyse their role.

B

The student does not make the lengthy discussion of censorship relevant to the title.

C

This final argument is fallacious. The conclusion does not follow at all from the fact that a newspaper chooses which words to use to describe an incident.

Check that claims you make clearly follow from the arguments you advance.

sense perception, reason and even in some instances, emotion. The ways in which these knowledge issues are addressed by society or even neglected to be addressed by society can give rise to larger ethical understanding of the authorities' plans for the future.

Other situations less life threatening, such as censorship of novels based on their context also hold the same intrusive knowledge obstructions. Limiting the range of a child's and adolescent's understanding of the world through the interpretation of a novel creates more limited understanding in their future …

By limiting the language that was used in this situation, the newspaper was in essence claiming that there is no such thing as truth in the matter.

This essay achieved 23/40, a grade B

D **C**

The student provides no reference for the source. The claim about Newspeak needs support and some examples.

Fully reference all your sources. Check that you give reasons and evidence in the form of examples.

D

The student equates "context" with "relativity" without any argument. As this claim reappears throughout the essay, underpinning the approach taken, it needs to be argued for and supported early on. This requires clarification of what the author understands by "context", "relativity" and "truth".

Key terms must be explored, and key claims supported, early in your essay.

In George Orwell's 1984, a language is created to eliminate uncertainty. All words that leave room for doubt and intellectual freedom are removed. Even in this new language, Newspeak, there remain a few words in which context is all. In a world where there should be nothing but the absolute, context still exists. If relativity exists, then does truth? Just because diverse circumstances may produce differing views does not mean that there is no truth. Objective truths are only interpreted and understood by context, not erased by it.

The claim that objective truths are understood by context is challenged by many people. They believe that relativism is evil, that there are firm truths in this world that never change despite the context. These people believe that black will always remain the colour black, even if it is called white in another language. If something is "morally wrong", it is wrong for everyone despite their circumstances. A truth that is fact to

A good attempt to explain (absolute) truth, though we are still not clear about its link to context.

Explain your understanding of the KI in the title as a whole, as well as individual terms.

A counter-example given, but not discussed very clearly. It also seems to be undermined later in the paragraph.

Construct your arguments carefully. Plan the key points before writing them in full.

The student makes several claims that need better reasons and support.

This argument is unsound. All that can be established is that both are successful in achieving the goal, but this does not imply they are correct (true).

Ensure the conclusions of your arguments do not go beyond what the argument establishes.

The student implies that meaning and truth are the same.

Maintain distinctions between key TOK concepts.

one person cannot be false to another; truth is absolute. However, this can easily be disputed when it comes to faith. Religion disagrees greatly in matters of practice and worship; yet, I and many people believe that all religions are essentially correct. As long as the religion leads towards love and morality, the religion must be true. This challenges the beliefs of those absolutists; if different faiths can lead to the same truth, then which one is correct? While a follower of Jesus Christ might attain God through Christianity, a follower of Karma might reach God through Hinduism. Both religions lead to the same goal, yet with different paths; both are correct. Differing situations and life experiences led to different religions. For example, in Christianity alone, there are hundreds of denominations; yet to be considered a Christian, one must be a follower of Jesus Christ. The objective truth remains; context just helps us to understand it. While absolutists would disagree, context is very important in interpreting objective truths.

In every area of knowledge, language plays an immense role. The words that are used to describe and help us understand the world around us are very important. Yet, one word can have a multitude of meanings. For example, the word "hot" can mean two different things, depending on the context. In one circumstance, it could mean that the atmosphere is sweltering. In a completely separate situation, a high schooler might be calling the new girl in town "hot", meaning beautiful. This one word's meanings never change; the two definitions will always exist. However, the meaning can and might differ due to different circumstances. Another famous homograph is the word "close". As a verb, the word means to shut something. As an adjective, the word "close" means nearness in proximity. There are millions of words in just the English language, and out of these words, there are thousands of them that have more than one connotation. A further example of the use of language is differing situations can be seen in the tone of the speaker. Sarcasm is a fantastic example to explain this concept. If the sentence, "You need to lose weight", was said to a tall, thin model, the effect would be humorous. However, if the same sentence was mentioned to a teenager with a weight problem, the effect would be horrendous. Sarcasm is used to say the exact opposite of what the words actually mean. The context in which the words are placed is what helps us understand the truth behind the words. Another example is shown in body language. Across continents, different gestures and motions mean completely different things. In some parts of the world, the "V sign" shown by the pointer finger and the middle finger raised and parted while the other fingers are clenched in a fist, can mean peace. In some European based countries, this same sign can mean something offensive and vulgar. While both definitions are correct, the culture and surroundings help define the meaning of the action.

The examples in this paragraph are well chosen to illustrate the effect of context on meaning. **B ↑**

Throughout history, most all events have two points of view, the victor and the loser, the aggressor and the victim, the saviour and the saved. Since history is written by historians hailing from either one of these sides or neither, history can be seen as subjective. However, no matter what the views of the different historians or personal accounts that are taken may say, the actual event occurred a certain way. The reality of the historical event can never be changed, even with propaganda and biased views. At the beginning of World War I, Belgium was invaded by the Central Powers. Belgium became the martyr for the Allies. "Poor Little Belgium" became a slogan for the Allied nations; it roused sympathy among the British and French, readying them for war. The British claimed that the Germans raped and mutilated Belgian women, cut the hands off of teenage boys and let children play with grenades. In truth, Belgium wasn't nearly as attacked as the Allies made it seem like they were. Later studies showed the both the Germans and the Belgians committed equal atrocities and the crimes rarely ever occurred. While propaganda and biases made the event into something colossal, the actuality of the invasion is still there. The truth behind "Poor Little Belgium" will always exist. Throughout history, there are many examples just like "Poor Little Belgium", even a few more just from World War I. Biases and propaganda, the context, can change the views the world has on a historical event. However, the event occurred a certain way, and that way is the truth

The student explores the effect of context on truth in the AOK history (and elsewhere, religion, the WOK language and the AOK ethics).

Make explicit links to AOKs and WOKs, where relevant. **A ↑**

There is no discussion of the distinction between historical facts and historical interpretations.

Revise what you have learned about the AOKs before writing about them in the essay. **A ↓**

Some claims contradict one another while others could be sharpened by discussing the difference between fact and interpretation.

Consistency and clarity of ideas and argument are essential for constructing convincing accounts. **C ↓**

In the vast world of ethics, context is truly significant. An act that might seem unjust to one person may be a part of someone else's regular life. In ethics all aspects of the situation must be examined thoroughly before a decision can be reached. The thought of being forced into a marriage decided by your parents to a man that is a complete stranger is frightening and completely unethical to a young woman living in today's America. However, if this young woman was of an Indian or Middle Eastern origin, an arranged marriage would seem completely normal and even expected in some families. The truth behind the matter really depends on the circumstances of it. If a man were shot while running away from a band of men, it would be considered homicide. If this same man was actually a famous criminal and he was running away from police men he had just assaulted, it would not be considered a murder. Ethics largely depends on the background information or the context of the situation. A thorough, ethical decision can only be

The examples chosen here do support the argument, though it might have been better to use more personal examples. **B ↑**

B D

The conclusion shows good insight and links back to the introduction, but the body of the essay does not develop and critique these ideas sufficiently.

Develop and expand your ideas with reasons, examples and argumentation throughout your essay.

determined after the context has been observed. A solitary event can be viewed thousands of ways, but the truth that is to be determined, will always remain the same.

Whether in ethics, history or everyday life, context plays a huge role in helping us understand the objective truths of the world. Without knowing the different circumstances and situations, even a reliable way of knowing may fail us. Objective truths will always exist in the world; they are eternal and can never disappear. However, to help us understand and interpret these truths, context must be there.

[Word count: 1208]

Examiner report

Criterion A: (6) The student's grasp of the central KI is set out well in the final two sentences of the introduction, and again in the conclusion, but the body of the essay does not expand and deepen it sufficiently. The explorations of AOKs history, ethics and religion lack depth and precision (for example in the failure to distinguish historical fact from interpretation). The account of the WOK language is weakened by a careless slippage between *truth* and *meaning*.

Criterion B: (5) The student does not consistently relate the essay to the title, and the essay does not have a strongly personal or reflective feel about it. Although they are used appropriately at times, the examples are not authentic enough because they do not seem to arise directly from the author's experiences. There are a few attempts to explore different perspectives, but they lack detail.

Criterion C: (6) The student attempts to support the major points, though the depth of analysis varies. Most of the arguments used are coherent, though there are occasional logical flaws. The few counterclaims introduced are not explored sufficiently. As the author had nearly 400 words in reserve, there was the opportunity for more detailed analysis.

Criterion D: (6) The organization of the essay is adequate. The introduction to the essay does not clearly address key terms or central concepts raised by the title, though this aspect of the essay improves, and the conclusion is well linked to relevant KIs. The body could do with a more consistent line of argument. There is some exploration of the meaning of key concepts, though *context* could be clarified better, and there is some confusion of *truth* and *meaning* at one stage. Some of the factual claims are dubious, and lack proper referencing.

Overall ...

The essay makes a strong claim: that truth must be interpreted and understood through context, but this does not mean that there is no objective truth. If this claim had been better argued, and the essay better planned, it would have scored more highly. However, it loses focus, partly on account of a lack of conceptual clarity, and partly because it does not engage in a sufficient depth of analysis and evaluation. How could the student have used a more personal tone in order to make the arguments more compelling? Could you suggest some more authentic examples, or better analysis or evaluation?

This extract was taken from an essay that achieved 20/40, a grade C (A = 5; B = 5; C = 4; D = 6)

(D) The student does not clarify "absolute truth" or "individual truth". What distinguishes individual truth from belief?

Give a developed account of any key terms you are going to use in a special way.

(D) The student gives only the general URL as a reference.

Use a standard, full method of referencing.

(D) The student does not make clear how his version is connected to the definition that he quotes.

Dictionary definitions must be used with care, and must be integrated into the essay.

(A) The student links the title's KI to an AOK (mathematics).

When you introduce an AOK, make the links to the title clear.

(B) (C) The student introduces mathematics as a possible counter-example to the essay's argument, supporting it with a (somewhat trivial) example, then counters it.

Identify and discuss opposing claims and counter-examples.

When using the word "truth" it is not the absolute truth we are referring to, but rather the individual truth, that truth which is meaningful to us. In this essay, unless otherwise defined, "truth" will refer to the concept of individual truth. The word "context" is defined as "the set of circumstances or facts that surround a particular event, situation, etc." (www.dictionary.com). For the purpose of this essay, this definition will be expanded upon to define context as the personal spin that is created through each knower's personal experience, point of view and background. It is the filter through which one perceives truth, and because this filter is so essential to our perception, it becomes an integral part of truth itself.

When speaking about relative truth or the possibility of multiple or partial truths, it is often brought up that in some areas of knowledge, truth is straightforward and unambiguous. For instance, in mathematics, most would agree that ten plus two equals twelve. It does not matter who is doing the problem, how the problem is approached, or where it is being done. Mathematics is often considered to be an area of knowledge that is independent of individual interpretation or context. What must be taken into account, though, is that the concepts and rules of mathematics are set up by humans.

This extract was taken from an essay that achieved 27/40, a grade B (A = 8; B = 7; C = 6; D = 6)

D The student sets out to define central terms such as *truth*; however, the muddled definition implies absolute truth (all that exists). It lumps together important TOK terms (truth, belief, knowledge).

Key TOK terms must be carefully explained, with related terms distinguished from one another.

C In asserting that there are multiple truths, the student contradicts his first claim for one all-encompassing truth.

In revising your essay, check for consistency.

A B The student puts forward a solid alternative view, supported by an authentic personal example (B), which links the AOK art and the WOK emotion (A).

Use examples from your experience to exemplify and support perspectives and ideas relating to the KIs.

Truth is all that exists, all the material, beliefs and knowledge in the universe and who knows what else. I write my response to the title based on this definition from a human perspective, the world in which we live, how the world exists around us and what it means to us, implying that if humans wouldn't have existed on this earth, the world I am referring to would neither have existed. Knowledge is part of the context the title refers to. Having context included in the definition of truth yields a multiple truth, although the title might imply one truth. Indeed, there are multiple truths because of context which varies for each individual or group.

Thus far I am assuming the existence of a multiple truth, but one could assume the existence of only one truth. Once during a music class I was moved by a piece, because of memories I had about the first time I heard it. … A friend then told me that the emotional reaction was all within me and couldn't be related to the song. According to him, everyone would hear the song in the same way, because there is only one record of it which always sounds the same.

This essay achieved 40/40, a grade A

B This detailed account of the student's struggle to find the meaning of "truth" shows reflective self-awareness.

'What is truth?' I was first challenged by this question in my TOK class. Although at first I was really confident with the meaning of the term 'truth', I ended up being confused. I believe we frequently take things for granted. These are ironically things which at first sound simple and essential to us, such as our identity (who am I). We tend to approach them as pragmatically. In the same manner we take the meaning of 'truth' for granted. If, however, we think about it we will end up realizing how complex it actually is. This leads us to our quest for the meaning of 'truth'; an endless spiral mind path in which the deeper we reflect on it, the more knowledge we obtain, but the less explicit the clause appears to be.

↑ D

In these two introductory paragraphs, the student identifies the two key terms and gives the reader a idea of how they will be understood, as well as indicating how the task of the title will be interpreted.

Use the introduction to clarify and show your understanding of the title.

↑ B

This excellent example is a very public one, but it is again made personal through the account of the evolution of the student's thought.

Link your examples to your own thinking and use them to develop argumentation and critical reflection.

↑ A

The influences of several WOKs are woven into this example very well.

Linking to TOK concerns is more effective if you integrate them into the discussion, rather than mention each separately, one by one.

↑ C

There are a string of questions here, but the student follows them through well by moving on to trying to answer them.

Argument by rhetorical questions alone is poor: always attempt to answer the questions you raise.

This, however, does not mean there is no such thing as truth. In my opinion truth exists. But not as one element but as many which are mostly subordinated by the 'thinkers' context. Everything we think, know and believe is a mere creation of our mind, which is build by many factors such as our memories, emotions, culture, reason, our perception and our language. As these form our 'context' and they differ from person to person, and as context is a mean to 'build truth', one can argue that context is essential but does not eliminate truth. In this essay I will analyze whether truth is universal or depends fully on the context.

A highly debated topic of whether truth is universal or depends on context is the 1948 UN Universal Declaration Human Rights (UDHR). Can our rights as human beings be universal although our contexts are so different? Who should be entitled to define them? Although the UN General Assembly was integrated by delegates from most countries, in my opinion the UDHR mirrors first and foremost Western mindsets and values. When I first reflected about this knowledge issue, I thought they were universal; or at least they should be. Certainly, I'm influenced by my personal context. Throughout my life I have been told by authority figures such as my parents that human rights (HR) are true and universal and that I, my family and friends will benefit from their implementation anywhere in the world. I am also influenced by reason, which at first does not let me see the logic of someone who deliberately disagrees with these rights. Therefore I've grown up valuing these rights because my reason, my emotions and authority dictate that these are 'true' and thus create a 'modern paradigm'. Although in practice HR are not fully practiced in Western societies, they are accepted as an idea of ultimate truth. However, what if they clash with legal, religious and/or cultural contexts in non-Western societies? Are these contexts then illegitimate? Are then HR truly universal or do they depend on the context in which they are implemented? Many Islamic countries have criticized the universality of HR arguing that they do not take into account non-Western contexts, highlighting the religious aspect. A UN representative of the Islamic Republic of Iran, for example, alleged that the UDHR is a "Western secular concept of Judeo-Christian origin, incompatible with the sacred Islamic sharia". Therefore, it cannot be implemented in Islamic countries without breaking Islamic law. Not only Iran, but other Islamic countries have striven to change either the UDHR or the use if the word 'universal'.

In other areas of knowledge such as the social sciences, specifically in anthropology, context is an important factor which constantly

Again, the student's engagement is shown through, not merely mentioning a personal experience (B), but also expanding on it and weaving it into the essay's inquiry (C).

The author's use of English is occasionally incorrect or unusual. However, this does not detract from the clarity of the writing, as the arguments are well constructed.

You can achieve clarity of writing even if you make occasional grammatical, spelling or word choice errors due to being a second language speaker.

A well-constructed argument takes the example and generalizes it, carefully linking it to the essay's central concern.

The judgment made about the connection between context and truth in art is backed up with reasons.

Ask yourself if you are giving the reader reasons to believe the claims you make.

influences 'truth'. My mother is an anthropologist and she often tells me how difficult this can be. She argues that the anthropologist's aim is not to find some abstract 'truth', but to interpret human behaviour in its own cultural context in order to understand it. Research findings are permeated by the researcher's worldviews and those belonging to the subjects under study. Let us take a young EZLN member in the Lacandon Jungle who sustains that he would rather die than accept that his ethnic group is not treated with the respect it deserves. Can we understand what he is feeling if we have not felt it before? This is called 'knowing by acquaintance' and is a factor which might challenge the pursuit of knowledge in anthropological research. When my mother uses a translator to interview indigenous people who do not speak Spanish, the message might be lost in translation because sometimes it is impossible to translate certain words or phrases that do not have an equivalent in the target language and its worldview. For example, the Spanish phrases 'te quiero' and 'te amo' are both translated into English as 'I love you'. However, 'te quiero' does not mean 'I love you' but expresses a different feeling which cannot easily be put into English words. These are central problems in any cross-cultural anthropological research which depends on the researchers ability to understand and interpret the 'other's expressions within their own cultural worldview and to reconstruct their underlying truth without imposing the researcher's rationale and truth on them.

In the abstract world of art both context and truth seem to conflict. Art seems to concur with Atwood's statement that 'context is all'. This is because art appears to be marked by a subjective nature and thus the knowledge acquired form it is subjected to the context of the observer. The subjective nature of art surfaced when many students in my TOK class found it difficult to understand what kind of knowledge could be acquired form art, probably because their idea of 'knowledge' was too concrete and narrow. This conflicts with the abstract nature of art and thus the abstract and personal knowledge which is gained from it. In the case of the visual arts, this message is abstract since art does not use symbols or active energy as a language, but a tangible and passive, yet expensive array of colors, figures, shapes and tones which by themselves, framed and hung on a wall, do not represent anything at all. The message is created by the interaction of the piece of art and the viewer who is influenced by all sorts of ways of knowledge—especially emotions—which are determined by the viewer's personal context. These have been increased and altered throughout the viewer's life by each single emotion felt, conversation spoken, impact digested, etc.

A

Again, the WOKs are woven into a discussion of context in art in a way that shows both an understanding of the KI, and an ability to see the contributions of the WOKs to that issue, rather than a list-driven mention of each in turn.

Let the inquiry drive your mention of the WOKs (or AOKs), rather than letting the list of WOKs drive your inquiry.

C D

This insightful passage carefully and clearly develops (D) a detailed account of the contextual nature of personal experience of the world (C), then neatly ties it back to the discussion of art.

Clarity of writing involves a step-by-step development of an argument (D), which will convey depth and detail (C).

D

A rare conceptual slip: is the author claiming that interpretation is the same as truth? More clarity as to what "expressions of truth" means would be welcome.

A

The focus throughout the essay has been firmly on the relation of context to truth, using both terms as explained in the introduction.

A

The student shows a subtle understanding of the central KI the title raises, which is consistent with the arguments and accounts developed in the essay.

Be aware of the complexity of TOK issues, and deal with it throughout your essay.

creating a mixture of every bizarre thing possible. This fusion comes to life every time the senses are used. When you open your eyes what you see will be related to this mixture or personal context creating a personal response. This is exactly what happens when you look at a piece of art. The message acquired will not necessary coincide with the message the artist had in mind when drawing the piece, but a message created by the personal context's interpretation. This is what makes it unique. Every individual will then craft his/her own truth according to his/her personal context (Beautiful isn't it?). Therefore, truth exists in art, but not as a single truth. Each piece of art will inspire as many expressions of truth as different viewers create when watching it.

A good example is Picassos' "Guernica" which created different interpretations and therefore expressions of truth in different historical contexts. I showed the painting to some of my friends and asked them what message they received from it. Almost all of them found the piece absolutely ugly. After doing further research I realized that this is a common way of seeing this mural today. Many present day viewers do not feel any emotion since their experience does not relate to the historical context of the painting. Their interpretation contrasts sharply with the one it inspired when it was painted in 1937 during the Spanish Civil War, right after the bombing of the Basque village of Guernica by German Luftwafe. 'Guernica managed to create a major impact'. Clearly, Picasso intended to send out a strong massage influenced by his emotions, as well as his personal and the general historic context. Josep Lluis Sert remembers the reaction of the public when the piece was first exposed. "The people marched in front of the piece in silence, as if they noticed that (…) the piece was a premonition of the consequences of the world war, (…) a sea of pain and death". The viewers interpreted the painting according to their personal and historical context, i.e. their emotions about the suffering of the Spanish Civil War. This reaction illustrates the connections between the historical context and the message that leads to a specific truth, a truth that differs sharply from that obtained from my classmates in the XXI century.

In quite different contexts, human rights, social sciences and the arts, context has proven to be an influential factor in the pursuit of knowledge. It is evident that at least in these areas context influences but does not eliminate 'truth' as a general concept. I would argue that truth is neither totally universal, nor is it fully determined by the context. Furthermore, context highlights truth and makes it admirable and interesting to such an extent that hundreds of IB students are at this instance writing about it. In the case of my essay, context can also be interpreted as a personal and unique account of an individuals' ways of knowing. It works like a poison, a glass of emotion, some past experiences, a handful of language and a spoonful of culture. Now stir it, drink it and let it influence your thinking through life.

[Word count: 1593]

Bibliography

"El Guernica—Pablo Ruiz Picasso. La historia del cuadro mas famoso del siglo XX"

http://blog.innerpendejo.net/2006/10/el-guernica-pablo-ruiz-picasso-la.html, (19/11/07)

Littman, David. "Universal Human Rights and Human Rights in Islam". Midstream, February/March 1999.

http://mypage.bluewin.ch/ameland/Islam.html (17/11/07)

"Pablo Ruiz Picasso", http://tierra.free-people.net/artes/pintura-pablo-picasso.php (19/11/07)

Word Reference: Spanish English Dictionary

http://www.wordreference.com/es/en/translation.asp?spen = quiero (8/12/07)

Examiner report

Criterion A: (10) From the early development of the key concepts underlying the title onwards, the student's strong grasp of the KI is demonstrated. It is a special mark of this essay that quite a few TOK factors (especially the WOKs) are not dealt with one after the other, but are rather woven into the developing argument precisely where they are relevant. This interweaving of ideas, when well done, is far more effective in showing how they are linked and compared.

Criterion B: (10) Throughout the essay, the voice of the knower shines through strongly, be it in the very personal tone of the writing, in the account of the author's TOK journey, or in the way the examples are shown to matter to the student. The student completely weaves examples into the developing argument, so that they not only illustrate points made, but also advance the argument. There is a highly reflective tone, and the student is clearly aware of the effect of context on his own thinking. In each AOK mentioned, the differing perspectives of others are clearly laid out.

Criterion C: (10) The level of argumentation is consistently high. The student supports all his major claims with well-linked reasons and analysis. His examples are also fully integrated into the argument (see also B), as are the TOK elements (see also A). The author shows a great deal of insight, through developing detailed and deep accounts. The counterclaim to the universality of human rights is sensitively explored.

Criterion D: (10) The essay has an excellent structure, both at the micro level of specific arguments, and overall. The introduction sets up a claim that is consistently explored and leads directly to the conclusion. Despite occasional language errors, the writing is always clear, backed up by careful consideration, and consistent use, of the key concepts. Sources are referenced at the end of the essay.

Overall …

The student sets out early on in this essay the way they are going to respond to the title and they maintain this consistent line throughout. The voice of the student is very clear, and the KI is analysed and discussed in detail, with good consideration of alternative perspectives. The few minor imperfections are not sufficient to require penalties on the criteria. Use the essay planning flow chart in order to decide how you would respond to this title and the KI which it presents. Does this KI apply to the certainty of any aspects of your own knowing and knowledge? Does it apply to any contexts in which you have found yourself?

This extract was taken from an essay that achieved 33/40, a grade A (A = 8; B = 8; C = 8; D = 9)

The anecdote in this essay extract is highly personal (B), involving WOKs emotion and reason. The AOK history (A) is integrated with careful analysis, linking it to a central theoretical point in the essay, the idea of two truths (C).

Examples from the writer's own experience are powerful when they are linked clearly to the developing argument and to relevant TOK concepts.

However, I feel that along with what actually happens in a situation, there is an entire other truth dealing with emotion. When my mother passed away last Christmas, I felt the most intense emotions of my life: [lists emotions]. I could tell you the truth by saying that my mother passed away, but you wouldn't feel those things, you would 'know' through reason. You wouldn't feel the truth about what happened. Those feelings were very true for me and mean so much more than that short, simple statement.… To me it isn't important that my friends know that my mother died, it's important that they know what I felt, what I went through. This idea of two truths can be connected to Tim O'Brien's "The Things They Carried". In this novel, O'Brien makes the distinction between storey truth and happening truth. Storey truth, we are told what will make us feel what the author felt regardless of whether the storey actually happened. In happening truth, O'Brien simply gives historical facts.

This extract was taken from an essay that achieved 34/40, a grade A (A = 9; B = 8; C = 8; D = 9)

An example in point is the various geometries. In Euclidean geometry, Euclid's 5th postulate that two lines are parallel if they are always equidistant, stretching infinitely far, is considered true. Non-Euclidean geometry disregards this postulate, creating a new environment for the mathematician to work in. It is possible to argue that the two contexts' incomparability invalidates *any* truth concerning the general behaviour of lines and planes. However, they represent separate mathematical realities, and thus the existence of one should not deny the other truth if the proofs within each context coheres with its own reality.

> **C**
> The student constructs the argument here carefully, taking into account a counterclaim (signposted by "it is possible to argue"), yet concluding that this does not invalidate the general position.
>
> Counterclaims do the best work when they provoke more careful reasoning in order to take them into account.

Ultimately, I believe that a crucial element of truth is its compliance with *reason* and, in the case of human or natural science, perception. Even if I am to claim knowledge by emotion, which cannot be proved empirically and perhaps does not require it, a rational explanation for that emotion will likely give it greater meaning, further validating its truth.

> **B**
> The student articulates a clear personal position, with an expansion that illustrates a subtle understanding of the interplay of three WOKs.
>
> Independent thinking and personal reflection can be shown by making, and elaborating on, judgments concerning how WOKs and/or AOKs are interrelated.

[From the introduction]: There are several theories that aim to determine which factors are essential in judging truth, and what constitutes sufficient evidence to warrant something being referred to as "true", but as a very wide philosophical concept there does not currently (and may never) exist one definition that incurs a wide consensus, and as such I will not attempt to conclusively define truth here. This essay will examine the truth of knowledge in economics and mathematics and the circumstances under which knowledge is acquired and applied in these fields. These contexts impact the certainty, correspondence to reality, coherence and pragmatic value of that knowledge, factors that often accompany truthful statements, and by which truth of knowledge can be judged[1]. To what extent must these factors be fulfilled in order to claim truth, and is this extent attainable? …

> **A** **D**
> The introduction sets up the essay well: it states clearly how "truth" will be understood (though "context" is ignored), sets out the essay's approach (D) and clarifies how the title's KI will be understood (A).

[1] R Abel, *Man is the Measure*.

> **D**
> Despite the fact that this book appears properly in the bibliography, the lack of a page number means the reference cannot be easily traced.
>
> All references should contain sufficient detail for the reader to easily trace the original.

[The conclusion]: In short, context *is* all. Contexts are often necessary for both acquiring and evaluating knowledge and ultimately determining truth. This may put in question either the universality of knowledge, such as in mathematics and ethics, or its correspondence to reality, as in economics and again mathematics. The issues of ambiguity in language and the need for consistency also come to light, particularly when considering the rigorousness of mathematical formulations and the inherent difficulties in defining emotion-laden words. Furthermore, the truth in mathematical proofs and economic models are validated by their coherence as well as by their pragmatic value. Ultimately, I believe that generally if a model or theory can be applied to a situation where it

> **B** **C** **D**
> The conclusion shows the candidate's original weaving together of the AOK topic matters covered (B), in a carefully constructed argument that claims no more than the essay justifies (C), referring back to the matters raised by the introduction (D).
>
> Use the conclusion to draw together the argument of the essay, with explicit reference back to how the introduction set it up.

is relevant and coherent, it can be seen as truthful. Absoluteness is not a reasonable requirement. After all, as there is no absolute definition of truth, perhaps it is not unreasonable that truth itself is contextual.

You should be able to:

☐ understand what can help you unpack your selected title; the following flowchart is one way in which this can be done.

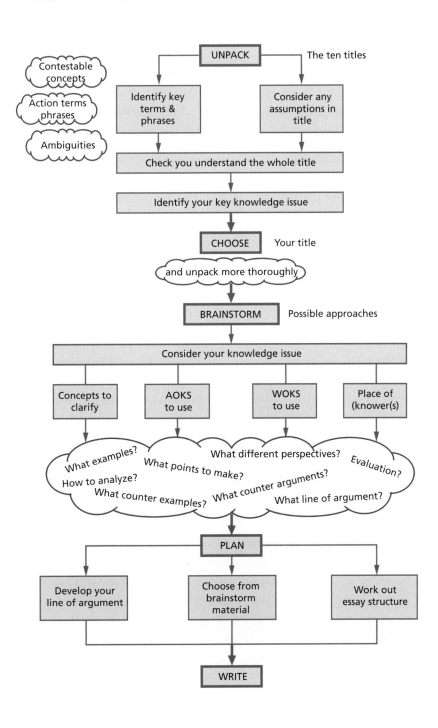

5. The TOK presentation

"The presentation takes place less in abstract-land and more in reality [than the essay]." (Morgan)

Showing others a bag of your own

The other, internal, part of your assessment for TOK is the presentation. If the essay is like unpacking, redesigning and repacking a stranger's bag, the presentation is yours from the start. It is like bringing a special, custom-made bag that you chose and packed for yourself, and pulling out of it the stuff you put in it. You and your classmates will each choose and present an interesting, substantive real-life situation (we expand on what this means in the next section) and explore a knowledge issue that arises from it. The presentation is marked by your teacher and the marks are submitted to the IB.

You can do your presentation by yourself, or as part of a small group. Your presentation can take many forms: it need not be a traditional talk, and it **must** not be merely read out (use flashcards rather than a script). Think about whether it might include a game, a simulation, a reading that you dramatize or an opportunity for some audience input. Additionally, a group presentation might include an interview, a debate, a role play, a chat show discussion and so on. Music, film, YouTube or TV clips can support your presentation, perhaps embedded in a MS PowerPoint® display. However you choose to package it, remember that this material should be an integral part of your TOK inquiry, not a replacement for it.

Figure 4

Your presentation serves two purposes. While the assessment purpose will probably loom largest in your mind, it is important that you do not lose sight of the other: your presentation is an integral part of the TOK course. Your classmates should learn more about TOK from your presentations, as you should learn from theirs. Although you will not be marked on your presentation skills, do have a thought for your classmates and try to make it an enjoyable as well as an intellectually stimulating experience!

The IB places no limit on the number of presentations you may give to the class, though practical constraints in your school usually mean you will only have a few opportunities. Nor do you have to do it at a particular time within the course—it can be early or towards the end—though again, in practical terms, you are likely to be able to give a better presentation after you have covered most of the course. Your highest mark will be the one submitted.

The presentation process

You might be tempted to grab the first likely looking topic and start writing a script, but we suggest that you approach the task in four stages:

Choose your focus ➔ **Brainstorm** the elements to include ➔ **Plan** out the presentation ➔ **Give** the presentation

We will concentrate mostly on the first of these stages for two reasons. First, we believe that if you choose your focus carefully, developing the real-life situation and knowledge issue from it thoughtfully, then you are very likely to do a good job of the rest. Second, the brainstorming and planning steps are similar to those for the essay, so you can look back at our advice for them in "Chapter 4".

Before you read on, you might like to watch one or more of the presentations on the DVD that accompanies this book. That will give you an idea of how other students have approached theirs, and our advice might then make more sense to you.

Choosing your focus

Your first idea for the focus of your presentation can come to you in a variety of forms. Maybe you already have a knowledge issue in mind, or a topic from your academic studies or the broader social world. Perhaps you have identified a real-life situation that you think has TOK implications. Whatever your starting focus, the IB requires that you develop that focus in a particular way. Your presentation must identify and explore a knowledge issue raised by a substantive real-life situation that

is of interest to you. Note the two important elements: what the nature of the situation you use is, and how you must develop and deal with a knowledge issue arising from that situation. We'll start with the nature of the real-life situation.

Interesting: find a situation that involves issues that matter to you. If you are working alone, look at your own interests. You may be fascinated by different people's attitudes to heavy metal music, or love the powerful use of language by your favourite poet. If you are working in a group, look for what you have in common: take time to discuss possibilities, so that every member can make a positive contribution. For example, one group might find that they all have parents who work in health-related fields (some mainstream, some alternative) and hence decide on exploring the efficacy of homeopathy. Another might be made up of residents of the school's boarding house, and decide to investigate how to live harmoniously in close quarters with others who are different.

Substantive: your situation should have substance, so that it raises an important knowledge issue. Trivial knowledge claims are unlikely to lead to deep TOK considerations. It is hard to be clear cut here, because some people can find a serious knowledge issue in even the most unpromising-looking situation, but you are unlikely to get much out of the claim in your primary school mathematics book that $1 + 1 = 2$, or the Louvre's catalogue claiming that the *Mona Lisa* is art. Better related situations might be a mathematical savant's claim that numbers have colours and personalities, or a claim that the graffiti that appeared on the school's wall is art.

Real-life: the situation should not be one you made up just for the TOK presentation. "Real-life" should not be interpreted to rule out such sources as incidents in novels or films: you and your classmates see these in your real lives. Rather, the situation must be one you have come across in your own experience that has implications for how you, and others, act in your own lives. Your own experience here is widely understood to include your personal life, your studies at school, your reading of books, papers or magazines and watching of other media and so on. Literature, films, songs, TV programmes and so on frequently raise knowledge issues of central concern in our real lives. On this interpretation, Shakespeare's depiction of Romeo's suicide because he "knows" Juliet is dead is as real life as George W. Bush's claim of victory in the war in Iraq, or your witnessing of a homeless boy stealing food from a big supermarket.

Situation: when you actually give the presentation, you should start with specific happenings or events, and not with an abstract question or issue. If what your group decides to look at is something like "is emotion the enemy of reason?", then find an appropriate situation to initiate your presentation, rather than starting it by asking this question. So, even if your interest is first sparked by a large issue such as the relation of emotion to reason, look for a specific incident, news story or similar to ground it in real life, such as a news story of environmentalists being injured trying to stop a whaling ship from killing whales. Although it is by no means essential, there is a good case for finding a situation in which you have been personally involved. Come back to the situation regularly in your presentation, to illustrate how the knowledge issues you are exploring relate to real life.

When you sit down to plan your presentation, it can be difficult to think of real-life situations to use, or even a topic that will lead you to a good real-life situation. Therefore, we recommend that, whenever you come across an interesting or puzzling situation, which makes you think "there is TOK in that!", you should make a note of it as a possible presentation starter.

> What interesting, substantive real-life situations might make a good presentation for you?

Dealing with your presentation

"Don't just state facts!" (Jaclyn)

"My last presentation didn't dig deep enough; it was just giving out some surface information but not much of our own thinking." (Malcolm)

Once you have the real-life situation, what do you do with it? Maybe you have made presentations to your classes in the past. Note carefully: the expectations for the TOK presentation probably differ markedly from these in one important respect. In those, you were quite likely to be imparting information or maybe arguing for one side of a controversial issue. In TOK it is different: you will be exploring knowledge issues. We'll illustrate this point with a couple of examples: the building of the pyramids; and the ethics of a starving person stealing food.

In a standard informational presentation, your job would be to find out as much as possible about the building of the pyramids, and then to tell the class. You might describe in detail the ways the large blocks were moved, how the slaves were fed and what the purpose of the pyramids was.

A TOK presentation on the same topic would be marked low if this was all you did. Only a small, introductory section of your presentation needs to give us information like this: just enough so that we know what your topic is about. In our example, you might show a few minutes of a documentary of the building of the pyramids where claims about the moving of blocks, the slaves and the pyramids' purpose are made. This will set up your knowledge issue concerning how reliable the information in the documentary is. You might state it as: Are there equally compelling alternative interpretations of historical evidence?

In a standard presentation on a controversial issue, you would most likely argue for the answer with which you agree, or maybe even-handedly mention pros and cons. So, you might say a starving person ought to be allowed to steal food without punishment, mentioning their distress, the profits made by big supermarkets and so on. In a TOK presentation, you need to identify a knowledge issue, such as: In ethics, how can we know when it is acceptable to punish someone?

Clearly stating the knowledge issue you identified in your real-life situation is essential to meeting criterion A. The rest of your presentation should then explore this knowledge issue. During this second phase of the presentation, you need to show how you meet the remaining three criteria. You need to be able to discuss (in the first example) the underlying standards of adequacy of evidence, or (in the second) rationales for punishment, that could be advanced on both sides, and analyse them for adequacy. You are aiming to understand the knowledge issue and strive for at least tentative or partial answers.

Note that, since this phase ought to be the bulk of your presentation, you should not choose a topic that requires extensive information before your classmates can appreciate what the knowledge issue is. Indeed, reasonably common, well-known or easy to grasp situations are often the best for a presentation.

The relationship between the real-life situation, the identification of the knowledge issue, and the developing of approaches to the knowledge issue is shown well in the following diagram.

> How will you make sure that your presentation explores a knowledge issue?

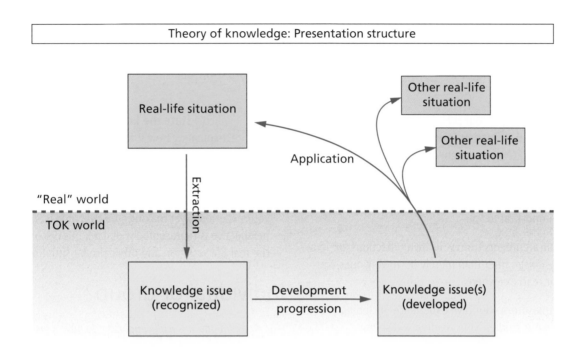

Figure 5

Unpacking the presentation assessment criteria

As is the case in regard to the essay (see "Chapter 4"), you need to have a sound understanding of the demands of the assessment criteria if you are to make sure your presentation meets them. Indeed, on the *Presentation marking form* (see the TK/PMF in "Appendix 2"), you will be asked to mark yourself against the four criteria straight after your presentation and to justify your mark briefly, so you had better know what they mean! Samples of these forms from previous students are given below (with the commentaries on the sample presentations). Your teacher will also mark you against the criteria and, after considering your self-marking, will decide on the mark to forward to the IB. You can score from 0 to 5 on each of the four criteria, for a total mark out of 20.

Please note that the forms used here are from the 2009 examination sessions. They may be altered for future examination sessions.

Criterion A assesses how well you have **identified a knowledge issue** that arises naturally and centrally from your real-life situation. You are allowed to consult with your teacher about the suitability of your planning, and nowhere is this more important than in choosing a good real-life situation and focusing on a good knowledge issue that arises from it.

Your presentation is part of the TOK course for the rest of the class: if you choose a sharp, fruitful knowledge issue, then the presentation is likely to strengthen their understanding and enjoyment of TOK.

- Pick your real-life situation carefully, and show clearly how your knowledge issue arises from it.

- Remember the hint that a knowledge issue can often be phrased "How do we know that … ?" (see also "Chapter 3" on knowledge issues).

- Given the time constraints, focus clearly on one knowledge issue (as you develop it, you may possibly include a few closely related ones that it raises).

Criterion B is about how well you have **shown your understanding** of the knowledge issue you have identified (and any related, subsidiary knowledge issues) through developing and exploring it. Link your knowledge issue to relevant knowledge considerations you have gained during the course. Some examples are:

- the influence of the knower's attributes on their interpretation of your situation

- the role of relevant WOKs in creating knowledge about the situation

• the methods used by several AOKs in handling your situation.

This criterion is similar to the essay criterion A, so check out the advice we gave there for demonstrating the depth and breadth of your understanding.

For **criterion C**, ensure that your presentation **draws on your own experiences and reflective insights**. After all, you were free to choose the topic, so you ought easily to be able to personalize it.

• Show why the situation, and the knowledge issue, you have chosen is so important to you.

• Construct your arguments from your own reflections (or, in a group, discussions), rather than merely borrowing ones you have heard or read elsewhere.

• Choose examples from your own experience, including your everyday life, your studies, your reading and so on.

• Demonstrate why your audience ought to care.

This criterion covers similar territory to part of the essay criterion B, so look there for more advice.

Finally, for **criterion D**, you need to develop in some detail **more than one way of looking** at the knowledge issue. Here are some suggestions (you may not need to cover them all).

• Remember that you are looking for different approaches to the knowledge issue, rather than different opinions about the real-life situation.

• Consider how someone different from you might approach the knowledge issue: if you are presenting in a group, then you may find the differences between you.

• Explore any differences that using other WOKs or AOKs as tools of inquiry would make.

• If you are tempted to turn your inquiry into a debate between two opposing perspectives, remember that most knowledge issues are more complex than that. Aim to explore the similarities and differences of different approaches to the knowledge issue and seek to establish a broader understanding that might resolve or reconcile them.

• Show the wider implications by looking beyond the specific situation you started with to other related ones.

Again, essay criterion B includes a similar section.

Be prepared

Whether your initial idea for your presentation is a real-life situation, a topic or a knowledge issue, when you are planning your presentation, keep in mind the following structure.

• Make sure that you find an **interesting, substantive real-life situation**, and start your presentation by briefly outlining it.

• Next, explicitly **state the key knowledge issue** that you will explore, explaining how it arises from your situation.

• Finally, use most of your presentation time to **explore the knowledge issue** in relation to your real-life situation: demonstrate your understanding of the issue, drawing on your experience yet making sure that at least one other perspective is represented well. Link this discussion back to the real-life situation and other similar situations.

Individual or group?

"For presentations, it is really important to have a group of students who are diverse in their ways of thinking and who can contribute clashing and supporting ideas, because TOK is not solely about who is right but more about paradigms and ways of viewing certain issues." (Jaclyn)

Each presentation can be given individually or in a group. Which will you go for? There are advantages and disadvantages in each. Weigh them up and find what suits you.

If you are thinking of giving an individual presentation, consider whether you:

• already have a strong personal interest in a topic, probably arising from your own experience

• have thought through a distinctive, personalized approach, and can already talk about it spontaneously

• can cover different perspectives and arguments by yourself

• are sure that your situation and knowledge issue can be handled adequately in about 10 minutes, which is the maximum time per student in a presentation. If you think you will need longer, you really should look for a classmate (or several) who shares your interest.

If you are thinking of joining in a group presentation, consider these points.

• More participants mean more input and different perspectives are available within the group to work from.

• You will have a longer time to go into more depth: 20 minutes for a pair, and 30 minutes maximum if your group has three or more in it.

- You can set up skits, role plays or similar where different perspectives are presented by different participants (but avoid ending up with an "is so"—"is not" debate).

- The larger the group, the more you will have to negotiate and compromise, as you are sharing control, and the harder it might be to develop a coherent presentation that holds your audience's attention.

- Finding a real-life situation you all want to work with can be more difficult.

- Ensure that every group member has a substantial input to a unified presentation (over both planning and presenting)—don't just chop it up and give everyone a piece to do.

> Which do you think would suit your strengths better: an individual or a group presentation?

Brainstorming and planning

Once you have chosen what your presentation will be about, you need to brainstorm and plan. As with your essay, the quality of your presentation will reflect how well you have planned it, and the process is similar. We have talked above about the shape and features your presentation ought to have, but you will have to fill in the details. As outlined at the start of the chapter, remember that there are many modes you can use to put across your ideas—lectures, role plays, questions for (or participation from) your audience, audio-visual supports and many more—but that you are not allowed merely to read out a pre-written text. Brainstorm which modes of presentation might make your presentation informative and engaging. Brainstorm which elements of your TOK course are most relevant to your real-life situation, and what detailed points you may want to make. Consider possible examples and counter-examples, arguments and counter-arguments. Think about what your overall line of argument will be. Look back at the brainstorming section of "Chapter 4" for some further clues to what you should consider.

Now you can plan. Decide which bits of your brainstorm materials are good ones. Put all this material into a coherent order.

> What method of planning—a mind map, a spider diagram, a planning tool in a word processor, scribbling on scraps of paper, or some other—will suit you best?

You need to complete, and hand your teacher, a *Presentation planning document* (TK/PPD, see examples with some of the presentation commentaries below) **before** you give the presentation. Going over a draft with your teacher much earlier is a very good idea. Preparing your TK/PPD will aid you in your planning, making sure you are on the right track. This is not a script but a summary of your plan. It needs to make your thinking clear: the situation you are analysing, the specific knowledge issue, and an outline of the main points you will make, in one A4 page.

Your teacher can also use the document to assist in their marking should your presentation for any reason—overenthusiastic questioning from the audience, equipment failure etc—not go according to plan.

Be prepared

- Choose whether you will give an **individual or group** presentation, keeping in mind the advantages and disadvantages of each.

- **Brainstorm** and **plan** your presentation carefully.

- **Complete a planning document** that summarizes the specific points you will make.

- Remember, you are not being assessed on how slick and professional your presentation skills are, but on the **quality of your TOK inquiry** into the knowledge issue raised by the situation you have chosen.

Example presentations and feedback

In this next section, we give a commentary on nine TOK presentations from the past. You will be able to watch the presentation on the accompanying DVD, and read our comments on how and why marks were gained and lost. Armed with this information, you should be able to approach your presentation confidently.

For a number of the presentations, we also reproduce, and comment on, the students' *Presentation planning documents*

(TK/PPD), and their self-assessment from their *Presentation marking forms* (TK/PMF), which you will be able to compare with the teacher's marks. Some of these were originally handwritten; we have transcribed them without changing spelling, grammar or punctuation.

These are the forms that you must complete as part of your presentation. Some of the documents we show you here have been completed very well, and you can gain ideas from them about how to do your own. Some others are reproduced so that we can comment on things to avoid when you fill in these documents for your own presentation.

A word of warning: do not be misled by the surface feature of the stronger (or weaker) presentations. A high-scoring presentation can be done by an individual, a pair or a group, with or without the use of skits, MS PowerPoint® or other presentation methods. What is important is that the presentation addresses the criteria well, so watch these presentations, and read the commentaries, with your attention firmly on the way in which they meet, or fail to meet, the expectations of the criteria.

Within this presentation, the student raises an interesting knowledge issue, but merely reports on some human science research findings without digging into the TOK concerns that are raised, so that the question of how we can be sure is never really addressed.

Can we be sure if a serial killer is made or born?

[Presentation 1, from May 2008]

This presentation achieved 8/20 and received a grade E

Time	Comment
	The student . . .
0.15	**(A)** states the KI Clearly.
	A question which starts 'how can we be sure' clearly concerns a KI.
0.20	**(B)** asks a few relevant sub-questions.
	Understanding of the KI can be shown by identifying further related questions.
0.25	**(A)** fails to explain or expand further on the KI, or to present a real-life situation from which to derive it.
	You need to draw your KI out of a real life situation, then look at its meaning and significance.
0.45	**(B)** lists a summary of attributes of the serial killer.
	A list of facts, no matter how accurate or interesting, does not show an understanding of a KI.
1.50	**(B)** states a number of possible sociological factors.
	The KI raised would be better explored by asking how these factors were identified, and if the methods were reliable.
3.10	**(C)** relates a personal example of the sorts of feelings a killer may have.
	Drawing examples from personal experience illustrates personal engagement.

Time	Comment
3.40	**(B)(C)(D)** lists more attributes of serial killers found in research.
	Finding information shows some engagement, but the information must be analysed for its TOK implications, or linked to relevant examples. Information must be linked to TOK considerations, such as the methods used by an AOK to generate it, or the WOKs used in gaining it.
5.45	**(B)** restates the KI, contrasting the born killer with the made killer, then lists attributes of the born killer.
	Needs consideration of how we would know whether a killer was born or made.
6.50	Fields questions about the facts already stated.
8.40	**(C)** when asked about the KIs involved, answers by restating facts.
	Take the opportunity raised by questions to reflect on and deepen your TOK inquiry.
throughout	**(B)** fails to mention any AOK explicitly, or any WOK, or to address the questions of "being sure".
	Ensure that TOK concepts are at the heart of your presentation.
throughout	**(D)** takes only one perspective: the facts found by psycho-sociological research.
	Ensure that several perspectives are taken, and that they are explicitly compared.
9.20	End

International® Baccalaureate

TK/PPD

Presentation planning document

Submit to: **TOK teacher** Arrival date: **See below** Session

School number:

0	0				

School name:………………………………………………………………………………...…..…………

- Write legibly using black ink and retain a copy of this form.
- Complete this form in the working language of your school (English, French or Spanish).
- Do not send to IB Cardiff or to the moderator unless you have been instructed to do so. Retain the forms until after the publication of results.

Candidate name: *Presenter One*

Candidate session number:

0	0							

Title of presentation: *Can we be sure if a serial killer is made or born?*

Please describe your planning for the presentation, either in the space below, or on an attached A4 word-processed page by completing 1, 2 and 3 below.

1. What is the real-life situation under consideration?

Serial killers

> The presenter identifies an issue, rather than a real-life situation that involves that issue. An actual example of a serial killer would be better.

2. What is the TOK knowledge issue that will be the focus of your presentation? (This must be expressed as a question).

Can we be sure a killer is born or made?

> The KI is clearly stated.

3. Write a summary in note form (for example, a bullet point list), of the way you plan to deal with knowledge issues during your presentation).

The key issues are assumptions, clarifying, and stereotyping. I will present my argument with a PowerPoint.

> This document lays out minimal planning. The three key issues identified here are not mentioned in the presentation. This section of the planning form should, at a minimum, spell out how the KI is going to be addressed, set out the structure of the presentation by detailing what specific points are going to be made with regard to each concept introduced, and identify the examples to be used. Clear planning will result in a focused presentation.

Presentation marking form (TK/PMF)

Presenter's assessment

Criterion	Comments/evidence	Achievement level (/5)
A	I believe and trust that I identify the knowledge issue	5
B		5
C	I was clear on personal involvement	5
D	I show different ways of perspective of this issue	3
TOTAL (/20)		**18**

> The presenter's self-assessment gives little evidence to support the achievement levels claimed. For criterion B, no comment is made at all. To be accurate in self-assessment, it is important first to understand the requirements of each of the criteria. Then, identify one or more specific parts of the presentation that show that you have met those requirements. If you try this before the presentation, and have difficulty identifying such parts, this is a sign that you need to modify your planning.

Examiner report

Criterion A: (2) The title of the presentation—can we be sure if a serial killer is made or born?—does state an intermediate knowledge issue, provided it is understood as question about kinds, and reliability, of evidence. However, this question is neither explained nor expanded. A real-life situation should have been used to raise the issue. The TOK implications of the question should not be ignored in the body of the presentation.

Criterion B: (2) A few sub-questions to the KI are asked, though no attempt is made to separate out factual questions from questions concerning the certainty of our knowledge. A presentation should dig beneath the facts to consider how we know them. Opportunities to identify the AOK from which they arise, or the WOKs which might be used to answer them, are missed.

Criterion C: (3) A powerful personal anecdote gives some idea of personal engagement, but no personal arguments are developed, and no further examples are given. The significance of the topic is assumed, but it should be explicitly demonstrated.

Criterion D: (1) Only a single perspective is represented: claims about the factors involved in becoming a serial killer. As the title mentioned two perspectives—born or made—the evidence that points towards each could have been investigated to see how credible it is, and how it is derived. Consideration could have been given to the possibility that there is some contribution from each.

Overall …

This presentation starts with a KI rather than a real-life situation—but then the KI is not explored. The one personal anecdote told (which could have been a good real-life situation with which to begin the presentation) is the only example used throughout. No TOK-related term is subsequently used explicitly, and it is hard even to find implicit mention. The presentation is almost entirely a listing of claims made by researchers, without any account of how these were discovered, whether they are sound, or where the information came from. Consequently, the "how can we be sure" part of the initial question, which makes it suitable as a KI, is never addressed. This presentation provides a good example of an unwise choice of topic. Since most people "know" more about serial killers from fiction than they do from reliable sources, the topic demands too much research from the student and the imparting of too much information to the audience before it is possible to tackle the underlying KIs.

Within this presentation, the student conveys a lot of information about instincts, gained from reading, but does not use this often interesting material to engage in a TOK inquiry.

Instincts

[Presentation 2, from May 2008]

 This presentation achieved 10/20 and received a grade D

Time	Comment
	The student . . .

0.05   starts with a broad general topic—instincts—followed by some definitions.

> Find a real life situation, and then explicitly state what KIs are raised by the situation.

0.35   implicitly raises the first KI: what type of behaviour counts as instinctive?

> The KI should be made explicit.

0.55   mentions that instincts do not involve reason.

> If you assert that two TOK issues are not connected, explore why.

1.00 ff   relates a lot of information about genetics and instincts from the AOK natural science, but …

Time	Comment
1.10 ff	**fails to explore these claims (for example are they justified? are the methods used to find them sound?).** Subject your knowledge claims to scrutiny, rather than merely state them.
1.20	**details an example of instincts involving a wasp.** Good examples could be used as the real-life situation—if unpacked and explored.
2.20	**does not make the relevance of the material on evolution clear.** All material in a presentation needs to contribute to the investigation of the KI stated early on.
3.00	**contrasts instincts with learned behaviour, through experience, leading to choice, but …**
3.10	**fails to expand on this contrast (for example by considering tacit vs explicit knowledge or the WOK reason).** Explore any contrasts claimed by introducing TOK concepts, WOKs or AOKs.
4.00	**mentions that instincts are "beyond thought" [see 3.10].**
4.15	**implicitly raises a second KI here: are humans subject to instincts?** Explicitly state your KIs, early on.
5.10	**introduces the controversy on human instincts, with two views stated, but …**

Time	Comment
5.45	**does not investigate the evidence for either side.** Weigh up arguments and evidence for competing views, and make a judgment about the KI.
6.45	**mentions the distinction of emotion and learning from instinct, but …**
6.50	**does not explore the relation of WOKs emotion and reason to instincts [see 3.10].**
8.10	**mentions that emotions may override instincts, but …**
8.15	**fails to use this to consider the implications for his first KI.** Be alert to all opportunities to link back to your KI.
throughout	**shows that he has done considerable research on instincts and so must have some interest in them, but …**
throughout	**reads out information which he does not seem to have written himself.** Information gathered needs to be reworked, to highlight the relevance to TOK. It is not permitted to read out an essay as a presentation.
throughout	**fails to give us any reasons to care about instincts, or to show any of his own thinking about them.** Showing personal engagement with the KI is essential.
8.40	End

International® Baccalaureate

TK/PPD

Presentation planning document

Submit to: **TOK teacher**   Arrival date: **See below**   Session

School name:……………………………………………………………………………………………………...……………

- Write legibly using black ink and retain a copy of this form.
- Complete this form in the working language of your school (English, French or Spanish).
- Do not send to IB Cardiff or to the moderator unless you have been instructed to do so. Retain the forms until after the publication of results.

Candidate name: *Presenter One*

Candidate session number:

0	0							

Title of presentation: *Instincts*

Please describe your planning for the presentation, either in the space below, or on an attached A4 word-processed page by completing 1, 2 and 3 below.

1. What is the real-life situation under consideration?

Instincts ————————

> This is an issue or topic, and not a real-life situation.

2. What is the TOK knowledge issue that will be the focus of your presentation? (This must be expressed as a question.)

How do instincts play a role as a way of knowledge?

The KI identified lends itself to a descriptive approach. Phrasing it differently ("Can instincts …") would open up a TOK inquiry better. The KI is not stated so clearly in the presentation itself.

3. Write a summary in note form (for example, a bullet point list), of the way you plan to deal with knowledge issues during your presentation.

So this presentation will deal with this knowledge issue as follows:
First the word "instinct" is going to be defined.
Second it illustrates how genetics play a role in instincts.
Third it will distinguish between instinctive actions vs learned behavior.
Fourth it will talk about the importance of instincts.
Fifth the role of instincts in human beings.
Sixth that reflexes are not the same as instincts.
Seventh it will talk about instincts in animals.
And last but not least there will be a conclusion to the whole subject.

This plan does give a structure to the presentation, but it is brief and fails to identify any TOK points that could be made. It is purely about conveying information.

Presentation marking form (TK/PMF)

Presenter's assessment

Criterion	Comments/evidence	Achievement level (/5)
A	Yes, it explained how instincts play a role in the way of knowledge	5

This KI is not explicitly mentioned in the presentation.

| B | Yes, it made us understand how instincts play a major role and have a high influence in animal and human life | 4 |

The comment does not show an understanding of the need to link to TOK concerns and the KI.

| C | Yes, lots of examples were given and explained in detail | 5 |

The examples need to demonstrate personal involvement.

| D | Yes it showed by talking about different controversial issues. It also relates to other areas of knowledge such as learned behavior. | 4 |

Controversies must be explored not merely mentioned.

TOTAL (/20) **18**

These comments do not demonstrate that the student has understood the requirements of the criteria.

Examiner report

Criterion A: (3) Despite the failure to be explicit, there are two interesting knowledge issues just below the surface of this presentation: How can we know what kind of behavior counts as instinctive? and How can we decide if humans are subject to instincts? The planning document mentions an even better one—Do instincts play a role as a way of knowing?—but this is not mentioned in the presentation. The student would have done well to choose one of these and make it central to the presentation. A real-life situation could have been found (such as the wasp example or, even better, one from the student's own experience) to set up the presentation.

Criterion B: (3) The student makes reference to a number of WOKs (emotion, reason, experience) and to the AOKs natural and human sciences, but consistently fails to explore the significance or links. Too many of the knowledge claims are made without any accompanying exploration of their status or connections to TOK concepts. The presentation is too heavy with information, and too light with inquiry, analysis and investigation.

Criterion C: (2) While the presenter has clearly done research, the material has not been personalized, and little attempt has been made to show why instincts matter: to him, or to the audience. The examples appear to be borrowed from the research done, not taken from his own experience. The presentation sounds as if it has been read directly from sources (which raises questions of academic honesty), rather than being reworked as a TOK inquiry.

Criterion D: (2) Some controversies in the field of instincts are raised, but there is little attempt to evaluate the support for each view, or to explore how we might make a judgment concerning them.

Overall …

Instincts are a very promising topic for a TOK presentation, but this presentation only occasionally, and briefly, touches on the TOK implications. The identification of relevant KIs is rather implicit, and an obvious line of inquiry—are instincts a separate way of knowing not mentioned in the TOK course?—is largely ignored, despite what is stated on the planning document. No real-life situation is introduced, from which to draw the KI. Doing so would have lessened the impression that we are merely hearing a lecture on the research findings concerning instincts: the presentation consists almost entirely of information transmission. Although much of the information is very interesting, this is not the purpose of a TOK presentation. Furthermore, the student comes perilously close to reading out a pre-written essay. This is explicitly banned in TOK presentations.

Within this presentation, the students conduct a mainly factual debate about the merits of the use of biofuels. Many knowledge claims are made, but they consistently miss the opportunity to subject them to TOK scrutiny.

The Use of Biofuels

[Presentation 3, from May 2008]

This presentation achieved 12/20, a grade D

Time	Comment
	The students . . .

0.10 state their title as a question (Are biofuels helping or harming the environment and our society?)—but do not identify this as the KI.

Your KI needs to be, not about matters of fact, but about the status of knowledge claims.

0.15 start a mock documentary, with each student presenting one side.

Make sure you have at least two perspectives.

0.25 give information about biofuels and some of its advantages.

Give only sufficient information to set up your KI and TOK inquiry.

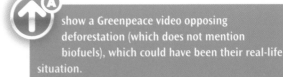

2.30 show a Greenpeace video opposing deforestation (which does not mention biofuels), which could have been their real-life situation.

Find a specific real-life situation to give your presentation a focus.

5.10 do not inquire into the status of the claims made in the video, many of which could easily raise TOK issues.

Take advantage of any one-sided case to explore the WOKs reason, emotion and language.

5.15 make the link between deforestation and biofuels.

Ensure everything you use is relevant.

5.35 state some of the problems of, and advantages gained from, logging, but fail to explore them.

Dig beneath disagreement to explore the perspectives they represent.

5.40 ff do not look at the methods of gaining, or the reliability of, the many factual claims they mention.

Use TOK concepts, AOKs and WOKs to question the factual claims you make.

7.15 engage in a factual debate on the overall environmental effects of the use of biofuels.

Look beneath the facts to the status of the knowledge claims.

9.20 present a graph on the effects of biofuels and discuss the implications for pollution, but do not link this to the AOK mathematics.

Look for opportunities to explore the AOKs from which your facts are derived.

Time	Comment
9.45	**B** state that "everybody knows" a certain fact about nitrogen oxides.
	Explore how people know, and whether that knowledge is sound.
10.25	**D** debate the effects of biofuel production on food availability and prices [see 5.35].
12.25	**C** talk about the pollution effects of biofuels in a rather mechanical way.
	Show why the issues you are discussing matter.
13.35	**C** say "We've given you all the facts", then …
	A TOK presentation is about an inquiry into knowledge itself, not about stating facts.

Time	Comment
13.40	**C** ask if audience is for or against biofuels.
	Engage your audience to emphasize the importance of your inquiry.
14.10	**C** give their own opinions.
	Stating your opinion, with the reasons you hold it, shows personal engagement.
15.15	**A** end with the question: is using biofuels ethical towards society as well as nature?
	A question that includes reference to an AOK is a better KI.
15.40	End

Examiner report

Criterion A: (3) No real-life situation is used to introduce the KI. The initial question—Are biofuels helping or harming the environment and our society?—is a factual one, and does not really open up knowledge issues. Nevertheless, there is a better question—is using biofuels ethical towards society as well as nature?—given at the end, and the presentation is of some relevance to this KI. A better presentation, with a narrower focus, could have been based on the Greenpeace video, used as a real-life situation.

Criterion B: (2) In persisting so long with the mock documentary, the presentation becomes focused on the statement of knowledge claims (facts), and seldom makes the move to exploring and investigating the status of those facts. This is well illustrated when one of the students says that "everybody knows" a certain fact. There is little explicit mention of TOK concepts, AOKs and WOKs, though they are brought up implicitly at times.

Criterion C: (4) The students do manage to convey some involvement in the factual issue, and have been able to organize a considerable amount of factual material into a coherent documentary form. Some of the examples used (for example the impact of using food crops for biofuels on Thailand) show personal engagement as knowers, though there could have been more. They offer their (joint) opinion at the end, and seek to involve the audience.

Criterion D: (3) Two perspectives (pro and anti) are given, though they are largely based on the factual claims. Each does have a significant case, and the summary shows a good attempt to draw upon both sides in forming a final opinion. However, the perspectives are insufficiently aware of, or grounded in, TOK concerns, and there is little attempt to show how the issues considered here might be applied to similar questions.

Overall …

This pair presentation is an informational presentation rather than a TOK one. The students do not have a sufficiently clear and focused KI. The question they start with is factual, though the restatement right at the end is a (poorly phrased) KI. Most of the presentation—a mock documentary—could have been used in a condensed form as their real-life situation (as could the Greenpeace advertisement). It presents a series of facts and claims, for and against using biofuels. A much shorter mock documentary of this sort ought to have been followed by a TOK inquiry into the claims made in it.

Within this presentation, the student delivers an interesting and well-constructed argument against the death penalty. While some TOK concepts are considered, the treatment of the knowledge issues remains largely implicit.

Death Penalty

[Presentation 4, from May 2008]

This presentation achieved 12/20, a grade D

Time	Comment
	The student . . .

0.10 — explains the death penalty and related terms.

Use a real-life situation to start your presentation, and draw the KI out of that.

Time	Comment

0.50 — explains why he opposes it; in doing so, he raises the KI—but only implicitly.

Choose a good KI, and be explicit about what it is. Make clear what you believe and why.

Time	Comment
0.55	attacks the death penalty as cruel and unusual punishment and states this is immoral (AOK ethics) and unjustifiable (WOK reason), but again is not explicit. Make your links to the AOKs and WOKs explicit.
1.00	fails to investigate how we know that the death penalty is immoral, or cannot be justified. Explore how you know that claims you make are true.
1.30	argues that it is not a deterrent, and gives statistics to back up the case. Back up your claims with reasons.
1.40	implicitly recognizes a different perspective (that the death penalty deters others), but misses the opportunity to give the reasons why others might believe this. Deal fairly with other perspectives, especially ones with which you do not agree.
2.10	refers to the use of the death penalty in crimes of passion and contrasts the WOKs emotion and reason [see 0.55].
2.30	argues that the death penalty denies human dignity, and hence is immoral, showing some individual initiative. Construct your own arguments where possible.

Time	Comment
3.00	points out the practical problem that it may kill an innocent person, and gives a very general example. Use specific, original examples to show your personal involvement.
3.40	refers to the denial of human rights, without explaining why this is a bad thing [see 1.30].
4.00	states the application of the death penalty is emotionally driven, ignoring context, and argues that we can't justify execution on emotional grounds [see 2.30].
4.40	implicitly recognizes another perspective in arguing that the death penalty contradicts the purpose of punishment: rehabilitation. Explicitly state any other perspectives you deal with.
5.00	argues that the death penalty is in contradiction with the anti-violence stance of the state. Make references to AOKs and WOKs explicit.
throughout	largely fails to address the obvious alternative perspective: that the death penalty can be justified. Always consider at least one other perspective.
5.15	does not invite questions. A question time is a chance for you to deepen your inquiry in response to issues you may have treated a little shallowly or unclearly.

Examiner report

Criterion A: (3) The presentation has a solid KI—something like: what evidence could help us decide whether the death penalty is ethical?—at its core, but it neither sets this up with a real-life situation, nor states the KI explicitly.

Criterion B: (3) The KI is dealt with, somewhat one-sidedly, in some detail. A sufficient range of AOKs and WOKs are introduced into the discussion, though it is too often left to the audience to recognize them. The discussion would benefit from the links and arguments being made more explicit.

Criterion C: (3) Although the presentation uses a number of reasonably individual arguments, there are no specific examples. The student does seem to feel strongly about the issue, but he could use examples and more detailed arguments to put this across more clearly.

Criterion D: (3) The approach to the issue is quite one-sided: against the death penalty. Some opposing approaches are acknowledged, but usually only to attack them. There is no attempt to see why others might believe them. The various strands of the case against the death penalty can be seen as taking somewhat different perspectives (ethical, rational, practical etc.), though this is not made as explicit as it ought to be.

Overall …

This presentation is an example of a talk which does not well fit the requirements of a TOK presentation, as it merely discussed the rights and (especially) wrongs of capital punishment. As a different type of presentation with different aims (say, to argue one side of a moral question) it would be very strong. First, the presentation starts, not with a specific real-life example, but with a general issue: the death penalty. Rather than being an exploration of a KI raised by the death penalty (and no KI is explicitly identified), it advances an argument against the use of the death penalty without considering the case for. A suitable KI might have been "how can we know if we are justified in using the death penalty?". In arguing his case, the student identifies the impact of a number of AOKs and WOKs of relevance, but this is usually done too implicitly, and without sufficient exploration of the status of the knowledge claims made. As the presentation is just over half the recommended length, there was plenty of time for a deeper inquiry, more focused on TOK issues.

Within this presentation, the student raises an interesting question from the specific real-life situation of a young Thai woman who is trafficked to Australia to work as a prostitute under conditions of virtual slavery.

Human Trafficking: How does tainted knowledge affect human trafficking?

[Presentation 5, from May 2008]

This presentation achieved 14/20, a grade C

Time	Comment
	The student . . .
0.20	outlines the story of Deng—a real-life situation.
	Start your presentation with a real-life situation (but don't read it straight from the screen!).

Time	Comment
1.10	relates the situation to the bigger issue of human trafficking, through defining what it is.
	Set up your KI by expanding on the situation and linking it to wider concerns.

Time	Comment
1.20	**(↑ B)** links the situation to the AOK economics (a human science).
	Identify which AOKs, WOKs or other TOK concepts can be linked to your KI.
1.30	**(↓ B)** does not deepen the inquiry by looking for subsidiary KIs in economics.
	When introducing an AOK, make sure you inquire into KIs, such as the reliability or relevance of the knowledge gained through that AOK.
1.30	**(↑ D)** considers the positions of both the victims and the traffickers.
	Different perspectives can be shown by considering how different participants view the same activity.
2.40	**(↑ A)** raises the KI—the role a lack of knowledge (by traffickers and by victims) about what they are doing—plays in their decisions. It would be better to phrase it as a question.
	Identify the KI drawn from your real-life situation.
2.50	**(↓ A)** might have been a little more clear and explicit about the KI, giving it more prominence.
	The KI is central to your presentation: highlight it.
3.15	**(↑ C D)** gives another real-life example of a trafficked woman.
	Examples help to make your KI more immediate, emphasizing the importance of your KI. They can also introduce another perspective.

Time	Comment
3.35	**(↑ B)** generalizes the example to show the economic impetus to trafficking.
	Make the links between your examples and your KI clear.
3.40	**(↑ D)** links the situation to AOK ethics.
	Making links to other AOKs introduces new perspectives and allows connections to be made.
3.50	**(↓ D)** does not take the opportunity to deepen the inquiry from the ethical perspective.
	Explore the implications of looking at your KI from a different perspective.
4.10	**(↓ B)** lists facts about slavery and subsequently gives statistical information on trafficking.
	Facts, on their own, do not deepen an inquiry into knowledge: they must be explored from a TOK perspective.
5.10	**(↑ D)** raises the question of whether the statistics are reliable …
	Questions about reliability of knowledge claims are vital to a TOK presentation.
5.20	**(↓ D)** but does not explore issues of reliability of statistical information [see 3.50].
5.30	End—Questions

Time   Comment

deals with the issues somewhat theoretically, with only two examples that are not explored sufficiently.

Make sure your interest and involvement in the KI is obvious.

5.40

in response to a question, explains why the issue matters to her.

Use any opportunities given by audience questions to deepen your TOK inquiry.

Time   Comment

6.25

agrees with questioner that human trafficking is the modern slavery, but merely by saying "yes" [see 5.40].

Examiner report

Criterion A: (4) The real-life situation, which is placed at the very start, is an excellent one. The KI is also excellent, though it might have been highlighted more when introduced. A little more time explaining the link between the real-life example and the KI would have made the presentation stronger.

Criterion B: (3) A grasp of the KI is shown through a structure that introduces three AOKs (human science, ethics and mathematics). However, a deeper exploration of, and inquiry into, these areas was needed.

Criterion C: (4) The presentation was a little dry and could have made clearer both the student's engagement and the significance of the subject. Nevertheless, the former was demonstrated in the student's response in the question time, while the latter was implicit in much that was said, particularly the examples.

Criterion D: (3) Different perspectives were represented particularly through the AOKs economics and ethics, and through the consideration of the perspectives of both the trafficker and the victim. Although there was some implicit comparison, the presenter could have picked up on opportunities to explore the connections and contrasts of these perspectives more deeply.

Overall …

This presentation starts off in excellent fashion with a real-life situation, and raises from it an interesting question about the role of incomplete knowledge in human trafficking, for both the trafficker and the victim. However, despite introducing some good links to AOKs, and asking some interesting supplementary questions, the student misses several chances to deepen the inquiry. As the presentation is quite short, there was ample time to do this. A well-constructed presentation was thus weakened by a lack of detail.

Within this presentation, the students raise the knowledge issue of whether we ought to believe in Darwinism or Creationism, through a specific real-life situation: the call in the USA for intelligent design to be taught in science classrooms.

Darwinism vs Creationism

[Presentation 6, from November 2008]

 This presentation achieved 15/20, a grade C

Time	Comment
	The students . . .

0.15 give the title of their presentation, which implicitly contains their KI.

State the knowledge issue clearly, preferably after introducing your real-life situation.

0.25 introduce their real-life situation: the teaching of intelligent design as science in school.

Choose a specific real-life situation that raises your KI.

0.30 do not expand their real-life situation sufficiently.

Outline your real-life situation clearly and show how your KI arises from it.

0.40 outline their own paradigms (or backgrounds)—features that might bias their views.

Explicitly acknowledge your own approach to your KI.

1.20 define creationism, Darwinism and intelligent design.

Clarify the key parts of your situation, but do not spend too much time giving information.

Time	Comment

2.20 role-play a debate between a priest and a scientist.

Role plays can be a good way to introduce different perspectives.

2.35 contrast science and religion as sources of truth.

Using key TOK concepts is a good way to contrast AOKs.

2.40 do not dig below the surface of different ways to understand "truth".

Pick up any use of TOK concepts and expand on them.

3.20 raise the link between justification (WOK reason) and science (AOK) but do not explore it, here or later.

When you mention the relationship between a WOK and an AOK, develop it.

3.25 advance the case for the scientific view and then the case for the religious view.

Contrast different perspectives directly.

Time	Comment

4.40 ⬇ B — claim, without expansion, a link between science and explanation [see 3.20].

5.15 ➡ B C — make several interesting claims: that, if one knows the truth, then no proof is required, and that God created the means of scientific proof.

Interesting claims (C) should be queried and defended (B).

5.40 ⬆ B — discuss the role play, analysing arguments and identifying fallacies.

Self-aware reflection on the real-life situation is essential to a good treatment of the KI.

6.45 ⬇ B — identify but do not critique their assumptions: if we take one perspective (for example the scientific) therefore we are not objective.

Identify and explore your assumptions.

7.20 ⬆ B — link the WOKs reason and language by identifying emotive language (religion = virus, fairytale).

Identify and discuss interactions between WOKs.

8.50 ⬆ C — advance their own opinions on the KI, drawing on the discussion.

After considering possible answers to the KI, you can make your own considered view clear, and defend it.

Time	Comment

9.05 ⬇ D — state that science has the stronger position, but neither side has conclusive proof, without investigating why.

Defend judgments you make between perspectives with analysis.

9.15 ⬇ B — state that truth arises from within a paradigm, and that it is up to the individual to choose [see 5.15].

9.50 ⬇ D — mention the strength of scientific support for Darwinism, but do not outline or evaluate that support [see 9.05].

10.10 Conclude the main body of the presentation and invite questions.

10.35 ⬇ A — clarify their KI.

State your KI clearly and early.

11.15 ff ⬆ B — respond to several questions by discussing in further detail several WOKs and AOKs

Use audience questions to deepen your argument.

International® Baccalaureate

TK/PPD

Presentation planning document

Submit to: **TOK teacher**   Arrival date: **See below**   Session

School name:..

- Write legibly using black ink and retain a copy of this form.
- Complete this form in the working language of your school (English, French or Spanish).
- Do not send to IB Cardiff or to the moderator unless you have been instructed to do so. Retain the forms until after the publication of results.

Candidate name: *Presenter 6*

Candidate session number:

0	0							

Title of presentation: *Darwinism vs Creationism*

Please describe your planning for the presentation, either in the space below, or on an attached A4 word-processed page by completing 1, 2 and 3 below.

1. What is the real life situation under consideration?

Intelligent design being taught as science in American schools

> Reasonable real-life situation, though it could be made more specific, by referring to a particular school or district and filling in some detail.

2. What is the TOK knowledge issue that will be the focus of your presentation? (This must be expressed as a question.)

Do we believe in intelligent design or Science? Is intelligent design a science?

> Although these are reasonable KIs, they were not the ones mentioned in the presentation.

3. Write a summary in note form (for example, a bullet point list), of the way you plan to deal with knowledge issues during your presentation).

Religion VS Science

Resources

- *Documentary Richard Dawkins*
- *Matt's Dad (scientist)*
- *Elliot's "Dad" (Priest)*

This planning document reads more like a brainstorm than a plan. There are many good ideas here, but they needed to be organized into a running order. Some of the ideas did not make it into the presentation.

Points to make

- *Is a school morally responsible for advocating scientific/religious classes as truth*
- *Both lack sufficient evidence to be proven*
- *Recognise Paradigms*

Put these in the presentation order, and briefly map out how they will be developed.

Presentation

- *Intro to topic (i.e. recognition of paradigms, definition of terms Intelligent Design, Creationism and Darwinism)*
- *Role Play*
- *Show clip of argument*
- *Discuss Fallacies in each argument as well as knowledge issues*
- *Finish with personal opinion*

Arguments ———————————

Incorporate these in the plan (above).

Darwinism (Matt)

- *Religion is blinding society from the truth that we live in an age of science not religion (emotive language)*
- *Intelligent design being taught in a scientific context, this imposes religion upon the youth*
- *Religion is like a virus, plaguing the people of the world and preventing them from progressing in a scientific world (emotive language)*

Religion (Elliot)

- *Argue that religion is the be all and end all, there is no point in studying material things when it is god who created everything, including science (circular argument)*
- *It should be taught instead of the Darwinism theory because of the reasons previously stated.*

Presentation marking form (TK/PMF)

Presenter's assessment

Criterion	Comments/evidence	Achievement level (/5)
A	Knowledge issue could have been focused on more	4
	Accurate, self-reflective comment.	
B	Enjoyed role play, was good way to show arguments	4
	Need to concentrate on quality of the arguments rather than the enjoyment.	
C	Was a good example of personal views	5
D	Should have mentioned other points of view	3
	Two perspectives are sufficient, if well analysed.	
TOTAL (/20)		**16**

Examiner report

Criterion A: (3) The KI—ought we to believe in Darwinism or Creationism?—is made reasonably clear, though not stated explicitly during the main body of the presentation. They are able to express it more clearly in the question period. The real-life situation is briefly articulated, with some expansion and exploration through the role play. It could have been explained early, and the links to the KI made more explicit.

Criterion B: (3) Throughout the presentation the students make, sometimes explicitly and sometimes implicitly, a number of interesting claims regarding the relation of science, religion, several WOKs and important TOK terms such as proof, faith, evidence, explanation and truth. However, these opportunities for deeper analysis and reflection are too often passed over. They do a better job on the WOK reason, exploring a number of fallacies of reasoning.

Criterion C: (5) The perspectives of the two students as knowers come through quite clearly, conveyed in a number of ways. In explaining their own "paradigms", they link their inquiry to their upbringings and experiences. After the role play, they explain and defend their own positions on the issue. Finally, in answer to the first question, they speak about why this issue seemed important to them.

Criterion D: (4) Two different perspectives are clearly set out through the role play, and each is developed in some detail. The similarities and differences between them are a little less well explored, and a shallow assertion that it is merely a personal choice which you believe is neither analysed nor defended. There is a tendency to consider the two perspectives as mutually exclusive, though this is acknowledged and explored a little in the question time.

Overall …

This pair presentation starts with a good real-life situation and develops it through a role play. However, they rely on their scripts to a degree that is in danger of breaching the TOK rules. By connecting to their own upbringings, they are able to show their personal involvement. The role play is quite rich, and raises quite a number of interesting knowledge claims (which could be more explicitly stated). However, the opportunity to analyse these is too often missed, both in the role play itself and in the discussion of the role play (with the exception of some solid analysis of arguments and fallacies). As a whole, the presentation lacks a consistent focus, and this springs in part from a failure to be sufficiently explicit about the KI, and partly from a failure to structure their plan. With 20 minutes available for a pair presentation, there was time to do better. The pair are fortunate that they are asked questions that enable them to come back and expand their analysis later. They do use several good techniques to acknowledge their knowers' perspectives and bring them to the fore.

Within this presentation, the contentious moral issue of honour killings is treated with sensitivity and fine awareness of complexity. The student is admirable in her ability to balance an even-handed consideration of diverse perspectives with coming to a well-supported and principled personal view.

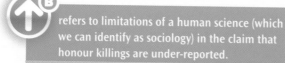

[Presentation 7, from May 2008]

 This presentation achieved 17/20, a grade B

Time	Comment
	The student . . .

0.20

avoids stereotyped or simplistic views by recognizing that honour killings occur in religions other than Islam and are at times carried out on men.

Show personal insight through careful analysis.

1.25

implicitly refers to three possible KIs: what are the effects of culture and education on how humans interpret a situation?; how is evidence used to justify accusations of wrongdoing?; and what are the evidential bases for the claim that there are honour killings? None are stated clearly and explicitly.

Choose a solid KI and make your statement of the KI prominent.

1.30

does not start with a real-life situation, but rather with a topic and some implicit knowledge issues.

Derive your KI from a real-life situation.

2.25

refers to limitations of a human science (which we can identify as sociology) in the claim that honour killings are under-reported.

Show awareness of methodological difficulties in AOKs, backed with reasons.

Time	Comment

2.50

gives a brief and succinct account of the cultural and historical roots of honour killings.

Provide necessary information without taking up too much of the presentation to set up the TOK inquiry to come.

3.30

recognizes the difficulties of separating out the interaction of religion and culture.

An understanding of the complexity of the KI can be shown through acknowledging the complex and ambiguous connections between AOKs.

3.55

comments that considering the KI as an instance of violence against women helps avoid the hasty generalization of a racist interpretation.

Show your personal insight into the poor use of the WOK reason by identifying fallacies.

4.20

discusses emotion and its effect on reasoning, and then on the interpretation of visual perceptions.

Show your understanding of the complex interplay of WOKs—but name the WOKs explicitly.

Time	Comment
5.10	**D** discusses two possible outcomes in exploring the effect of education: more sympathy to women, or more ability to justify anti-woman judgments. Recognizing two contrasting effects shows an ability to grasp differing perspectives of the same issue.
5.55	**B** refers to the role of scientific investigation in providing evidence for ethical inquiries (but without labelling the AOKs). Acknowledge the interaction of AOKs.
6.00	**C** shows awareness that (women's) testimony may not be true, and that (men's) reasons given may not be the true reasons. Dig below the surface to show personal insight into the ways knowers are affected by their context and beliefs.
7.05	**B** explores the interpretation of religious texts, and how this interacts with factors previously mentioned. Explore the role of WOKs and their interactions with the attributes of knowers.

Time	Comment
8.30	**C** acknowledges the possibility that her gender may render her biased, leading to the recognition that men can suffer from honor killings too, and that women can carry them out. Show awareness of how one's own personal attributes as a knower can influence one's beliefs.
9.50	**C** summarizes by drawing together the points made and making the case that we ought to work to stop honour killings. Base your personal response to the KI on a careful consideration of many factors.
throughout	**D** addresses the topic through the lenses of several WOKs (emotion, reason, language) and AOKs (human sciences, culture and religion, natural science, ethics). Make your links to TOK concepts varied, subtle and explicit.
10.30	End

Examiner report

Criterion A: (3) Although the presentation, overall, addresses several strong KIs, it could have led into, and identified, them much more explicitly. It starts with a general topic (honour killings) rather than a particular real-life situation: choosing an account of a specific honour killing would have enabled the presenter to set up the KIs clearly.

Criterion B: (5) The presentation shows considerable insight into the complexity of the topic, analysing the relevance, and interaction, of a number of AOKs (human science, natural science, ethics) and all four WOKs. There is also a fine sensitivity to the effects of the attributes of knowers on their beliefs.

Criterion C: (5) The presenter on a number of occasions expresses thoughtful, reflective insights into the material she is considering. She is well aware of complexity, yet makes a strong case for action.

Criterion D: (4) The presentation shows a fine appreciation of the complexity of the issue, considers the views of different knowers, and looks at several (implicit) KIs through many AOKs and WOKs, though too often without using TOK terms explicitly when doing this.

Overall …

This presentation's major flaws are structural. First, the presenter ought to have started with a specific real-life situation involving an honour killing, and then proceeded explicitly to draw out the KI: there is insufficient focus at the start. Second, the discussion could have brought the relevance to TOK more to the surface by using TOK terms more often. As your presentation is part of the TOK course for your audience, you should ensure that you make the TOK relevance clear at all times. If these flaws are set aside, then the presentation is insightful, with the presenter exhibiting a very strong ability to dig deeply into the issue, and to understand its complexity. Perhaps its strongest feature is her ability to represent the views of those with whom she does not agree, yet to argue strongly for her own conclusion. With more attention to the technical requirements of a TOK presentation, this could have gained a score of 20/20.

Within this presentation, the students start from the real-life situation of four different "national views" drawn from their research into the attitudes and beliefs of students in their boarding house. This leads to their KI, after which they explore how the TOK considerations can aid their colleagues and themselves in avoiding a stereotyped reaction to others.

> Living in an international boarding house: How do we accommodate difference across cultural backgrounds?

[Presentation 8, taken from 2008]

This presentation achieved 19/20, a grade A

Time	Comment	Time	Comment
	The students...		
0.15	explicitly tell us their KI (though they call it a topic) and then link it to the real-life situation.	0.20	choose a KI that is perhaps a little too tied to the real-life situation. It could investigate understanding across cultural difference in general.
	Clearly identify the real-life situation and the central KI early.		A good KI looks beyond the specifics of the real-life situation from which it arises.

Time	Comment

Time	Comment

0.30 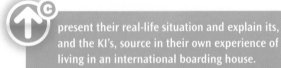 present their real-life situation and explain its, and the KI's, source in their own experience of living in an international boarding house.

You can highlight your knower's perspective by including an account of how and why you came to choose your topic.

0.45 have collected real-life data by interviewing their colleagues, but they have shown a good awareness of issues of confidentiality by making the answers generic and anonymous.

Be aware of the dangers of presenting highly personal information—one of which is that it can obscure the more general considerations that make a good KI.

0.45 give an extended example by having each of the four nationalities answer several questions. This section could, perhaps, have been a little shorter. However, a group presentation allows time for developing a more extended real-life situation while still allowing plenty of time for analysis.

In order to set up your treatment of the KI, amplify your example sufficiently to provide some good examples to pick up later.

0.45 gathered answers by interviewing different boarders.

Finding how different people react to the same situation will introduce different perspectives.

5.15 follow the extended example with a commentary on each segment, drawing out some of the stereotypes.

Make the links between your real-life situation and your KI, to move from the situation phase to the analysis phase of your presentation, and remind the audience of your KI.

5.45 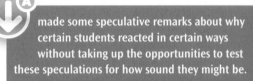 made some speculative remarks about why certain students reacted in certain ways without taking up the opportunities to test these speculations for how sound they might be.

Speculative assertions ought to be subjected to scrutiny.

7.15 make explicit the differences between the data gathered from two cultural groups.

Highlighting different perspectives from within your real-life situation shows your grasp of connections.

7.45 identify and give a commentary on the concept of paradigms, tying the situation to TOK issues surrounding knowers.

Move from the details of your situation to an account of more abstract TOK concepts.

8.00 recognize that different people from the same paradigm can still have different viewpoints—a point that is returned to (see for example 11.15, 12.55, 18.50).

Show a thoughtful, personal approach by avoiding either/or judgments.

8.45 in the food examples, the students do not read from notes.

Being able to talk about your subject without reading notes shows a clear personal involvement and understanding.

9.00 talk about "how we grew up".

Make a clear linkage between theoretical points and your own experiences.

Time	Comment

9.30 comment that certain food is "so weird for us".

Make clear, personal statements of different perspectives on the same situation.

10.00 start an extended analysis of how informal fallacies contribute to stereotyping in the boarding house.

Use WOKs explicitly to analyse the situation.

10.30 draw on their own experience to give counter-examples of hasty generalizations.

An effective counter-example drawn from your own experience will always be better than a made-up or borrowed one in demonstrating a different perspective.

11.30 give an extended example of special pleading from their own experience.

Personal examples can both show the knower's perspective and advance the analysis of the KI.

13.20 appeal to influence of cultural backgrounds (the knower) and circumstances (sense perceptions) on the WOK emotions.

Weave together the influence of several TOK concepts.

14.00 carefully explain the fallacy of loaded questions with an example well tied to the situation.

Formal definitions can be clarified with a well-chosen example—especially effective if clearly drawn from the real-life situation.

Time	Comment

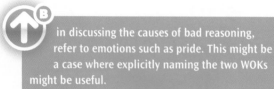

15.00 in discussing the causes of bad reasoning, refer to emotions such as pride. This might be a case where explicitly naming the two WOKs might be useful.

Link together WOKs.

15.15 suggest conciliation as a way to overcome problems arising out of clashing paradigms.

Practical advice shows personal engagement.

15.50 comment on the links between language difficulties and laziness.

Identify connections between a WOK and an attribute of knowers.

16.30 comment on judgmental tendencies and claim we reason better when we look from multiple viewpoints but form our own opinion.

Showing insight into your own behaviour demonstrates how TOK has influenced your perspective.

17.00 develop an argument that language limitations affect not just communication but also limit our minds and emotions.

The distinction between language and mere communication, and the recognition of the far-reaching effects of language, show a deep grasp of this WOK.

Strive for depth in your analysis.

18.15 analyse how backgrounds affect the interpretation of greetings.

Turn your theoretical discussions to a different, but still related, example to show understanding and introduce more perspectives.

Time	Comment

18.45 consider solutions to the KI, by drawing together succinctly the main conclusions of the presentation.

Demonstrate your understanding not merely by repeating your conclusions, but also by showing their applications.

20.15 show some entertaining counter-examples to stereotypes raised in the real-life situation, tying the presentation together and reinforcing the main message.

Make your points in an entertaining fashion.

Time	Comment

21.30 talk about changes to their personal actions on the basis of their investigation.

Demonstrate that your presentation has not merely been a formal requirement, but has also touched your life.

International® Baccalaureate

TK/PPD

Presentation planning document

Submit to: **TOK teacher**   Arrival date: **See below**   Session

School name:..

- Write legibly using black ink and retain a copy of this form.
- Complete this form in the working language of your school (English, French or Spanish).
- Do not send to IB Cardiff or to the moderator unless you have been instructed to do so. Retain the forms until after the publication of results.

Candidate name: *Presenter 8*

Candidate session number:

| 0 | 0 | | | | | | | | |

Title of presentation: *Living in an international boarding house: How do we accommodate difference across cultural backgrounds?*

Please describe your planning for the presentation, either in the space below, or on an attached A4 word-processed page by completing 1, 2 and 3 below.

1. What is the real life situation under consideration?

Role play: four generic interviews of generalisations created by interviews we conducted.

> A real-life situation drawn from their own experiences, but generalized to protect confidentiality.

2. What is the TOK knowledge issue that will be the focus of your presentation? (This must be expressed as a question.)

How do we embrace cultural differences after living in a diverse community of many cultural backgrounds? A discussion on how to live in the boarding house.

> Identifies the key KI explicitly and succinctly—but could it be broadened?

3. Write a summary in note form (for example, a bullet point list), of the way you plan to deal with knowledge issues during your presentation).

Outline:

1. Discussion: Issues raised by the interview—Stereotypes
2. Cultural Paradigms—complications and implications
3. Fallacies—complications and implications

    a. Hasty generalisation
    b. Ad homonym
    c. Circular reasoning
    d. Special pleading
    e. False analogy
    f. False dilemma
    g. Loaded questions

4. Causes of bad Reasoning—complications and implications

    a. Pride
    b. Prejudice
    c. Laziness
    d. Ignorance

5. Language—complications and implications
6. Customs (Greetings)—complications and implications
7. Conclusion: now that we have identified all the complications, what is our solution? Summary of actions to take
8. "Breaking cultural stereotypes"

Link to the KI.

Could have briefly identified what the complications are, and the implications to be considered.

Better—the specific fallacies are identified.

Could state more explicitly that these relate to the WOK emotion.

Again, a few key points to be made would improve the plan.

Overall, a very good planning document that follows the formal requirements. The use of numbered sections provides an excellent structure, and lays out clearly the connections of the presentation to the TOK concepts to be considered. A little more detail in places might make it even better.

Presentation marking form (TK/PMF)

Presenter's assessment

Criterion	Comments/evidence	Achievement level (/5)
A	Cultural mesh → real life boarding house, international relations	5
B	Considerations of solutions and point of view of different cultural stereotypes	5
C	Four video interviews, multiple opinions and analysis	5
D	Discussion of topic with various perspectives and discussion of implications	5
	TOTAL (/20)	**20**

This assessment by the students shows a good grasp of the requirements of the four criteria. It identifies a few of the points appearing in the presentation, for each criterion, that contribute to the group's meeting of that criterion. However, they could have mentioned specific instances for criterion D.

Examiner report

Criterion A: (4) The presentation was structured so as to state the KI (though they called it a topic) clearly: How do we embrace cultural differences after living in a diverse community of many cultural backgrounds? They explained well how it arose from a real-life situation of obvious interest and importance to the students involved. The KI could have been more generalized to explore the implications of their discussion on cultural difference in general.

Criterion B: (5) Three elements show their high achievement on this criterion. First, they analysed well a number of key TOK concepts (knower, culture, paradigm, reason, emotion, language) in relation to their situation. Second, they showed the interaction between these elements, demonstrating their grasp of the complexity of both the situation and the TOK analysis of it. Finally, they continually linked their more abstract points to the situation through a series of well-chosen personal examples and counter-examples.

Criterion C: (5) In quite a number of ways—in the choice of examples and counter-examples from their own experience; their obvious enthusiasm; their ability to speak fluently at times without notes; their ability to construct personal accounts and arguments (occasionally quite striking)—the students demonstrated their personal knowers' perspectives on the topic.

Criterion D: (5) The students introduced a number of different ways of contrasting perspectives: from their own cultural backgrounds (and those of others); through different WOK lenses; from different lengths of time in the boarding house; among others. They also demonstrated the ability to draw together these perspectives and consider a number of the interesting ways in which they interact (for example cultural background and personal attributes; reason and emotion, language and emotion).

Overall …

This group presentation clearly arose from a matter of great personal import to all the students involved. The structure is excellent, in introducing a real-life situation, drawing a clear KI from it and using TOK concepts to analyse it in depth. It is interesting that they did not always explicitly identify the TOK points they were making (for example, at 13.20, they did not state that they were giving an example of the interaction between knower-based upbringing and cultural background, the sense perception-related circumstances one is in, and the WOK emotional reactions one has). Signposting such connections can be a way of drawing your knowledge to the attention of your teacher, but doing it too much can make your presentation sound piecemeal. A sophisticated analysis that has just enough, but not too much, signposting shows a well-embedded understanding of TOK. Overall, this is a good example of a presentation that, by tackling a matter within their own and their audience's experience, did not get bogged down in researching and conveying a lot of information. Despite the local emphasis, the issues covered are of huge importance in the world—and this could have been explored a little more, if their KI had been stated more generally.

Within this presentation, the students use a series of skits to raise a number of factors related to the knowledge issue concerning the interaction of science and ethics. The skits involve characters who see the relationship between science and ethics differently. Each is followed by an analysis of the relevant factors.

Science and Responsibility: Does modern science take responsibility for its moral and ethical implications?

[Presentation 9, from May 2008]

This presentation achieved 19/20, a grade A

Time	Comment
	The students...
0.20	**A** clearly state the broad knowledge issue of the place of ethics in science.
	Ensure your KI is clear to your audience, but try not to make it too broad to handle in one presentation.
1.00	**A** use a television interview skit to raise more specific KIs.
	Draw your KIs from real-life situations.
1.50	**D** show awareness of complexity by comparing scientific atomism with two types of holism: Eastern and Western.
	Make connections and demonstrate perspectives by drawing on different cultures.
2.10	**B** use a specific example of the atomistic approach in genetic engineering to explain both atomism and a version of the scientific method (AOK natural science).
	Choose examples that illustrate your understanding.
3.30	**D** use a specific counter-example to show problems with atomism, and link it directly to AOK ethics.
	Using a counter-example can raise questions that allow you to bring in other factors.

Time	Comment
4.10	**D** draw attention to the place of AOK reason in science.
	Introduce your links to other WOKs or AOKs when they naturally arise.
4.40	**C** show a different scientific perspective (ecology) that includes ethical considerations.
	Show that there are different approaches possible even within a single AOK.
4.55	**C** back up the claim of damage from scientific inquiry with the example of BT maize.
	Choosing good examples from your studies or other experience is a way of showing your perspective
5.40	**D** contrast the holistic approach to scientific inquiry with strict control of variables [see 4.40].
6.00	**D** discuss the possibility of combining atomism and holism.
	Show your understanding by not merely identifying opposing ideas, but also seeing to what extent they are compatible.

141

Time	Comment
7.00	**B** analyse key concepts: holism and atomism.
	Identify the key concepts behind your KI and explicitly analyse them.
8.45	**C** foreshadow the key ideas in the skit to come.
	Be explicit about the concepts your situations are raising.
9.00	**D** identify possible clashes of science and ethics, through ideas of objectivity and subjectivity.
	Use key concepts to identify features of the AOKs or WOKs worthy of exploration.
11.00	**D** compare the AOKs science and art (literature) for their abilities to understand social implications.
	Look at the different ways AOKs can go about achieving the same aim.
11.45	**C** illustrate their point with a skit drawn from literature [see 4.55].
14.30	**B** analyse key concepts, subjectivity and objectivity following the skit [see 7.00].
15.30	**C** defend the claim that scientific objectivity is based in a certain subjective mind set, with WOK emotional underpinnings, and link this to literary insights.
	Making fresh links between disparate areas shows your personal reflection.

Time	Comment
16.20	**C** contrast literary hypothetical situations with scientific hypotheses [see 15.30]
17.00	**D** present a parable about the link between scientific advance, applications and ethics [see 4.55].
20.40	**B** explicitly analyse the links raised in the skit [see 7.00].
21.00	**B** present a skit drawing together previous points about how to incorporate literary and religious insights to lend an ethical awareness to scientific research.
	An example that synthesizes many of the issues considered previously underlines your depth of understanding.
23.50	**C** summarize the commonality of purpose of AOKs science and ethics, with suggestions about how a synthesis can be achieved [see 15.30].

International® Baccalaureate

TK/PPD

Presentation planning document

Submit to: **TOK teacher**   Arrival date: **See below**   Session

School name:...

- Write legibly using black ink and retain a copy of this form.
- Complete this form in the working language of your school (English, French or Spanish).
- Do not send to IB Cardiff or to the moderator unless you have been instructed to do so. Retain the forms until after the publication of results.

Candidate name: *Presenter 9*

Candidate session number:

0	0						

Title of presentation: *Science and Responsibility: Does modern science take responsibility for its moral and ethical implications?*

Please describe your planning for the presentation, either in the space below, or on an attached A4 word-processed page by completing 1, 2 and 3 below.

1. What is the real life situation under consideration?

Approaches that modern science already takes to have responsibility for its consequences, and the approaches that modern science needs to take to be able to claim the responsibility for the medical and socio-political implications of its discoveries and work. This will be demonstrated through a series of sketches (Ayurveda Skit, two scientist skit, director of hatcheries, emperor skit and the religion skit).

> The sketches neatly turn some big and general issues into real-life situations. Two of them are taken from literature.

2. What is the TOK knowledge issue that will be the focus of your presentation? (This must be expressed as a question.)

Science and responsibility- comparing and contrasting the modern scientific method shown through genetic engineering to alternative approaches in traditional medicine, ecology, the arts and religion.

> The KI is stated more succinctly in the presentation than here. It ought to be in question form. Several subsequent KIs are identified in the plan below.

143

3. Write a summary in note form (for example, a bullet point list), of the way you plan to deal with knowledge issues during your presentation).

First Sub-knowledge issue: Comparing modern science and its atomistic approach towards fact with that of alternative medicine which has a holistic approach.

Atomism/holism- First Sketch:

- Traditional science compared to Modern Science around the basis of genetic engineering.
- Atomism provides us with 'universal' results and replicability.
- In Holism- evaluates all variables (the body, mind and soul are all regarded).
- Reike works only when the patient believes it will work.
- We will conclude that atomism allows a treatment of many patients rapidly, thus is better for short term treatment. While, holism gives a more complete treatment.

> There is a clear statement of the key points to be raised in this skit, and the KI they address.

Second Sub-knowledge issue: Comparing modern science and its objective approach to that of alternative subjective approaches.

Subjectivity/Objectivity- Second Sketch:

- Discusses the need for subjectivity in science as a method to be introspective about the implications of science.
- Subjectivity integrates aspect of ethical, emotional, and spiritual implications.
- Subjectivity allows us to see the horrors that are created through objective science- eg. Frankenstein.
- Objectivity makes science empirically provable and observable.
- The detachment from emotional subjectivity enables scientists to be manipulative as seen in the director of hatcheries skit.
- Objectivity looks at the mineral level- it is methodological as seen in the director of hatcheries skit where the professor creates a new 'efficient' world (the categories of human kind that will make an efficient human race)—it brings out the principle of mass production of the human race.
- We will conclude that scientific objectivity is required at points as it allows data to be replicable yet can create dire consequences.

<u>*Third Sub-knowledge issue:*</u> *How can religion and the arts help us to deal with the issue of responsibility in science?*

Hierarchical/non-hierarchical:

- *Our Chinese parable skit talks of the evil that can be found within man and his ability to manipulate things around him.*
- *Arts and religion use emotion, subjectivity to be fully encompass that which they study.*
- *The visuals present in the power point presentations like Michelangelo's Creation of Adam and Eve shows the evil present in humans.*
- *We will conclude that religion especially can aid scientists greatly in understand the implications of their work.*

The presentation will talk about alternative methods that could add to modern scientific method so that it can be responsible for its implications. The alternatives that we will take were utilized subjectivity, emotion and a holistic approach to take responsibility for their actions. We will conclude that these methods could help scientists take responsibility for their implications.

An excellent planning document, though it is not necessary to write it out in full sentences as much as is done here. Point-form phrases are sufficient.

Presentation marking form (TK/PMF)

Presenter's assessment

Criterion	Comments/evidence	Achievement level (/5)
A	We compared aspects of modern science to evaluate its ability to take responsibility for its results.	5
B	Sketches and visuals were used to show both negative and positive implications of genetic engineering relevant to our lives.	5
C	Different perspectives were shown through the geneticist, ecologist and ayuvedist to show contemporary issues that relate to us.	5
D	Skits bring out different perspectives that could be addressed in the topic, for example, atomism/holism, objectivity/subjectivity.	5
	TOTAL (/20)	20

> In the cases of criteria A, B and D, the presenters have picked out one or two key points that show their understanding of, and ability to meet, each criterion. For criterion C, their comment is perhaps more relevant to criterion D—identifying places where their own perspectives were evident would be better.

Examiner report

Criterion A: (4) The presentation is very clear about the overall KI, though it is rather broad to be dealt with in detail in a presentation, so they have to break it down later. The students might usefully have drawn a more manageable KI from one of their real-life situations, rather than stating the KI first. Several subsidiary KIs are clearly introduced in this way, arising from subsequent skits.

Criterion B: (5) The presentation analyses the KIs raised in considerable detail, using a series of contrasting concepts (for example holism/atomism, objectivity/subjectivity) to throw light on the issues. It also includes a good range of AOKs and WOKs, very well integrated. Examples chosen are very relevant, highlighting the understanding.

Criterion C: (5) The presenters construct arguments that draw together many considerations in a way that clearly indicates considerable individual and joint reflection on the issues. The examples are drawn from their previous studies and experiences, and have been neatly chosen to illustrate or raise important TOK matters, as well as highlighting the importance of the main KI.

Criterion D: (5) Having characters in the skits represent differing perspectives assisted the presenters to meet this criterion very clearly. Contrasts were made not only between the perspectives from different AOKs, but also from differing approaches within a single AOK (for example systems-based ecological vs controlled variable approaches in science). Particularly impressive were the attempts to find ways in which the differing perspectives might be reconciled, or at least work together.

Overall …

This group presentation deals with a broad but clearly important KI: the connection between science and ethics. Although the KI is probably too broad and hence has not been dealt with fully, the presenters have used the extra time available to a larger group to address a range of underlying issues, while clearly indicating their connections to the main KI. A single presenter would focus on a more sharply drawn KI, such as one of the subsidiary KIs here. A particular strength of the presentation is the way the skits are used: they are well focused and then well analysed. Skits and examples do not explain themselves, commentary and analysis are necessary to draw out their relevance to the KIs, and to make their lessons clear. Incorporating two very relevant skits drawn from literature shows good connections between the TOK presentation and the presenters' wider experiences.

You should be able to:

- [ ] understand that the task of preparing and giving the TOK presentation is now much clearer. We have discussed the specific structure it must have, and how it differs from other types of presentations
- [ ] understand the process: choose, brainstorm, plan, present. You have been able to watch real presentations from past IB students, and read a commentary pointing out just where they gained and lost marks
- [ ] understand what the **presentation task requires** you to do
- [ ] understand why it is important to find an interesting, substantive **real-life situation**, and what counts as one
- [ ] understand the importance of explicitly stating a **knowledge issue** that arises from your situation
- [ ] understand what each of the **four presentation criteria** requires you to do in stating and exploring your knowledge issue
- [ ] decide whether to give an **individual** or to join in a **group** presentation
- [ ] **plan** your presentation well.

6. TOK assessment at a glance

Here, briefly, we summarize two crucial aspects of the TOK assessment tasks. First, we highlight the major differences between the essay and the presentation. Next, we boil down our advice into six essential suggestions: our top tips.

Know your way around

On any journey, it is always useful to have a general map that shows the whole territory, even if it lacks local detail. That's the purpose of the table below, which summarizes and contrasts the distinctive features of the essay and the presentation. For the full detail, you can read chapters 4 and 5: they are the local maps which contain considerable detail.

Be prepared

- Although both the TOK tasks were designed to allow you to demonstrate what you have gained through the TOK course, they do have different features and emphasize different capacities. Bear these in mind as you approach the tasks.

Essay and presentation: what are the key differences?

Feature	Essay	Presentation
Your product	A written essay with certain formal requirements	A live performance in front of the class (which may be recorded for verification)
Size of the group	Must be done individually (but you can seek advice from others)	Can be individual or a small group (up to five)
Your starting point	A title you choose from 10 supplied by the IB	An interesting, substantial real-life situation you choose for yourself
Knowledge issue	The KI is generally fairly *explicit in the title*—criterion A asks you to show you *understand* it	Criterion A requires you to *identify explicitly* the KI that arises from your real-life situation
Relation of the general to the particular	Starts with general concepts that you must analyse, both conceptually and through linking to particular TOK issues (criterion A) and examples (criterion C)	Starts with a particular real-life situation and moves to more general ideas: assessed by criteria B (understand KI) and D (different perspectives on KI)

Feature	Essay	Presentation
Personal perspective	Criterion B assesses how much your treatment of the title arises from independent reflection on the issue	Criterion C assesses your personal immersion in, and illustration of, the ideas covered in the presentation
Analytic skills	Explicit assessment of analysis, including support for your claims and consideration of counterclaims, in criterion C	Not explicitly assessed, though good analysis contributes to a successful presentation
Organization	Good essay structure, clarity, coherence and flow of argument assessed directly in criterion D	Apart from the requirement to start in a real-life situation, then identify the KI (criterion A), not explicitly assessed (but good organization contributes to a successful presentation)
Grasp of other perspectives	Show your awareness and grasp of other perspectives as part of criterion B	Good treatment of other perspectives is essential for criterion D
Referencing of sources	Must be done, if you draw on the words or ideas of others	Not assessed for a presentation but mention major influences in any audience handouts or on the PPD
Relation to TOK course	Your essay is done when the course is complete, and should showcase what you have learned	Your presentation is a part of the course: it should give other students a deeper TOK understanding
Who marks it	An examiner (who is also a TOK teacher) from outside the school	Your TOK teacher(s), taking into account the marks you give yourself

Top tips

We hope that this book will help throughout your preparation for your presentation and essay, but here are our top tips.

1. **Choose carefully** your essay title, or your presentation focus. For the essay, analyse all 10 titles first, so that you choose the one that best fits with your interests and strengths. For the presentation, choose a real-life situation, or topic, or knowledge issue that really matters to you but is also constrained enough for you to be able to treat in depth in the time available.

2. **Plan, plan and plan!** Before you start writing your essay, or detailed presentation, brainstorm, then plan, the main points you will make, the examples you will use, the different perspectives you will consider, the counterclaims you will explore and so on. Get your thoughts, ideas and lines of argument straight, and in order, **before** writing. Be specific and include enough detail so that someone else can see the complete skeleton of your argument. For the essay, structure the plan with an introduction, body and conclusion. For the presentation, structure it to start with the real-life situation, move to the KI that arises from it and then outline the presentation body and conclusion.

3. **Remember your TOK.** Draw on what you have learned in your TOK classes. If necessary, revise your notes or read a TOK text on TOK concepts, AOKs or WOKs etc that will be central to your work. But be careful! Don't just copy what the text or your notes say. The point is to remind yourself of the complexity of these areas, to get you thinking more deeply, and to ensure you don't ignore some key distinction or idea, or make some simple error.

4. **Personalize your work.** Choose a topic that you care about, and convey that enthusiasm. Think the issues through for yourself (but drawing from all you have learned in TOK—see tip 2). Choose examples from your own experience (your everyday life, your studies, your interests …). If a common example comes to your mind, look for a more personal or original one that will make the same point.

5. **Use your teacher.** Talk through your plan with your teacher before writing the whole essay or presentation details. Listen carefully to their advice and questions. It will be much easier for you to make important changes at the planning stage than to revise an already completed product. Nevertheless, use the opportunity to show your teacher your full essay draft as well.

6. **Know the criteria.** You are trying to convince the examiner that you have written a strong essay or given a convincing presentation. So, remember that they will be looking at what you have done through the lens of the criteria. Thus, while you are putting it together, you should use the same lens.

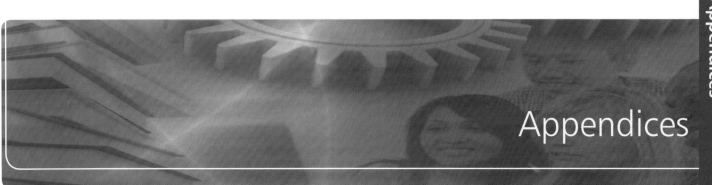

Appendix 1: Blank table for unpacking your essay title

One way to approach the unpacking and brainstorming stages of your essay is to use the table below. Use the first part for unpacking titles, and the second for brainstorming possible elements of your essay There are many other ways; choose a method that suits you.

Stage	Notes
Write in the title	
Unpack the question	
Identify key words and phrases	
Identify the contestable concepts to clarify	
Identify the action terms	
Identify any ambiguities	
Identify any assumptions in title	
Check you understand the title: write the sense of the whole title in your own words	
Identify the key knowledge issue you will address	

Brainstorm	Claim	Points to develop	Examples/counter-examples etc
How will you treat the main KI?			
Which AOKs and/or WOKs and/or facts about knower(s) will you consider?			
What contestable concepts need clarifying?			
What different perspectives will you consider?			
What will go in your introduction?			
What conclusion does all the above mean you come to?			

Appendix 2: Presentation marking form (TK/PMF)

 International® Baccalaureate

TK/PPD

Presentation marking form

Submit to: **TOK teacher** Arrival date: **See below** Session

School name:………………………………………………………………………………...……………

- Write legibly using black ink and retain a copy of this form.
- Complete this form in the working language of your school (English, French or Spanish).
- Do not send to IB Cardiff or to the moderator unless you have been instructed to do so. Retain the forms until after the publication of results.

Candidate name:

Candidate session number:

0	0								

Presenter's assessment

Each presenter should give themselves an achievement level for each of the four assessment criteria. Presenters should briefly justify the level they have given, in the "Comments/evidence" space provided.

Criterion	Comments/evidence	Achievement level (/5)
A		
B		
C		
D		
	Total (/20)	

I certify that this presentation was the work of myself (and my co-presenters, if applicable).

Candidate's signature: …………………………………………… Date: …………………

Teacher's assessment

In the "Comments/evidence" box, please indicate briefly why you have given each level.

Criterion	Comments/evidence	Achievement level (/5)
A		
B		
C		
D		
Total (/20)		

I certify that this presentation was, to the best of my knowledge, the work of the presenters named (with permitted teacher support).

Teacher's signature: ……………………………………………… Date: ………………………